Microwave Cookery
for the Housewife

Cecilia Norman

Pitman Publishing

First published 1974
Reprinted 1974
First paperback edition 1976
Reprinted 1977 (*twice*)

Pitman Publishing Limited
Pitman House, 39 Parker Street, London WC2B 5PB

Fearon Publishers Inc.
6 Davis Drive, Belmont, California 94002, U.S.A.

Pitman Publishing Pty. Limited
Pitman House, 158 Bouverie Street, Carlton, Victoria 3053, Australia

Pitman Publishing
Copp Clark Publishing
517 Wellington Street West, Toronto M5V 1G1, Canada

Sir Isaac Pitman and Sons Limited
Banda Street, P.O. Box 46038, Nairobi, Kenya

Pitman Publishing Co. S.A. (Pty) Limited
Craighall Mews, Jan Smuts Avenue, Craighall Park, Johannesburg 2001,
South Africa

ISBN: 0 273 01008 5

Text set in 11/12 pt. IBM Baskerville, printed by photolithography,
and bound in Great Britain at The Pitman Press, Bath.

G.125 : 17

Acknowledgements

The author wishes to thank R. E. A. Bott Limited, Voxdean Limited, Mealstream (UK) Limited, W. K. Thomas & Company Limited and Electric Catering Centre for technical information and advice; and Miss Mary Cathcart Borer for assistance with the text of the book.

Contents

Illustrations

1 Microwave Cookery at Home

During the 1960s the microwave oven quickly proved itself a valuable asset to all types of catering establishments, because of the extreme speed and facility with which pre-cooked meals can be re-heated ready for serving, and frozen foods thawed. For example, a frozen pre-packed meal which might take 45 minutes to reach a serving temperature in a conventional oven from the frozen state or about 20 minutes from a refrigerated state can be ready for serving after 1½ to 4 minutes from the frozen state or 45 seconds to 1½ minutes from a refrigerated state in a microwave oven, the times varying according to the power of the oven.

During World War II it was found that microwaves pass easily through rain, smoke and fog, all of which block light-waves. Their special properties made it possible for images of distant objects such as enemy shipping and aircraft to become visible on a radar screen. It was in the course of this radar research that the heating properties of microwaves were discovered.

Now microwave cookery is proving itself equally valuable in the home, not only for quick re-heating or for the thawing of frozen food but also for basic cooking. As these recipes will show, the microwave oven will save hours of time in cooking almost any items of food and in hastening the processes involved in the preparation and completion of a dish.

Microwaves have many of the same characteristics as light-waves. Electric light is generated in an electric light bulb but microwaves are generated from electrical energy in a vacuum tube operating as an oscillator called a magnetron.

Microwaves will pass through such substances as glass, porcelain, china, earthenware and paper. As they pass through without effect those substances will remain cool. When microwaves meet metal they are reflected from it and the metal also remains cool. But when microwaves encounter the moisture contained in food they are absorbed by it. The millions of molecules which comprise the food begin to jump about, rubbing against one another and causing friction. This results in massive heat, which forms the cooking process. It could be compared with the proverbial boy scout rubbing two sticks together to start his fire.

This is the reason that foods cooked by microwaves become hot much more quickly than those cooked in a conventional oven. In that form of cooking heat reaches the centre of the food slowly by conduction. That is to say the heat is applied to the outside surface of the food which passes to the next layer and so on until the centre is reached and cooking is completed.

With the advent of the microwave oven, a change in the technique of cooking has arrived. Microwave cooking is not an improved method of cooking by conventional means. It is an entirely new approach to the exercise, for it is a new method of introducing heat to food. The food is exposed to electro-magnetic waves and the heat is generated inside the food itself.

This calls for a certain amount of re-thinking on the part of the cook, just as the first gas and electric cookers did in the case of cooks who had spent most of their lives grappling with tempera-mental kitchen ranges.

The microwave oven is not designed to replace conventional cookers but should complement them. Few appliances are more than 70 per cent efficient. A vacuum-cleaner will not reach the edges of a fitted carpet unless an attachment is used. A freezer preserves food for only a limited time and some foods cannot even be frozen and returned to their previous state (e.g. strawberries). Other electrical appliances, such as a waffle iron, can be used only after they have been on for a time and become hot enough for use. Although some microwave primary cooking may seem slow, at least there is no 10-minute wait for the oven to reach the correct temperature. The ideal way of cooking is to use your conventional oven in conjunction with your microwave oven and your freezer. For example, when cooking Yorkshire puddings, which will not cook in a microwave oven, make a batch of them in your conventional oven, freeze them and re-heat when necessary in the microwave.

Although at the moment the microwave oven is mainly used for re-heating foods previously cooked by conventional means, this recipe book will show that it is not only possible but easier to prepare a great variety of dishes from basic ingredients. Do not think in terms of buying a tinned ready-made sponge pudding to re-heat, either by steaming on your conventional cooker or by re-heating in the microwave. It is cheaper to prepare the mixture yourself; you will then be sure that there are no added chemicals and preservatives. Beefburgers are so easy to prepare from minced beef, onion powder, salt and pepper. Just shape on a floured board and cook in the oven for 1 minute. The cost of the basic ingredients is at least halved. Crème caramel, which is obtainable in ready-mix form which needs no baking, can be left on the grocer's shelf. It is not the mixing of the eggs and milk that is difficult, it is the pre-heating of the oven and the long water-bath cooking that is tedious. Tedium is not a word applicable to microwave cooking.

Naturally you will need to practise. Once you have used an electric mixer and blender it is difficult to imagine how food preparation could have been done without them, but their use had to be learnt, and so it is with microwave cookery.

Microwave ovens are not radioactive. They have no connection with X-rays or radioactive fall-out. They simply convert electrical energy into radio waves, and they are equipped with safety devices which ensure that there is no risk of microwaves escaping into the room. The principle in every model is the same. The door cannot be opened while the oven is in operation. Once the door is opened the unit shuts off. There are also other in-built safety factors, such as various devices to check any leakage of microwaves through the door when it is locked and cooking is in progress. The primary door seals reflect the microwave energy back into the oven, and secondly there is a gasket made of materials which will absorb any possible leaking microwaves. If your oven has a drop-door, therefore, never rest anything on it or you may damage the door's perfect alignment and fit.

This safety factor is especially important in a home where there are small children. There is no electric hot-plate to burn their hands and no switches that can be accidentally turned on to produce fumes. There is a main switch now standard with all microwave installations; if this is switched off after use, no harm will come if the button on the oven itself is pressed accidentally. However, remember to keep half a glass of water in the oven when it is not being used so that there is something to cook for a short time if a child activates the oven, since the magnetron can be damaged if the machine is operated when empty. The oven can be damaged but not the child. A microwave oven is heavy and so it is virtually impossible to pull over. The doors are fairly stiff and require some strength to open. It is safer also for the half-awake husband cooking his own bacon: no burning himself with hot fat, nor will it matter that in searching for a bandage he forgets to switch off the oven, for the microwave oven having been pre-set to cook for a certain length of time will automatically switch itself off, so avoiding the acrid smells of burning pervading the whole house, to say nothing of the problems of cleaning a blackened frying-pan.

As the sides of the oven remain cool, food particles do not burn against them and the oven stays clean, needing only a quick wipe over with a damp cloth.

Many hours will be saved as a result of rarely having to clean spillage from boiled-over milk. Milk will boil over more readily in a microwave oven, but there is less chance of this happening if it has been programmed for a specific time and when it does boil over, as some day it surely will, you will only have to wipe over the oven base and the cooker will be ready for use once more.

Cooking odours, which often cling, will not be noticeable to visitors since the "smelly" part of the cooking can be carried out earlier in the day.

Microwave cookery virtually dispenses with the need for sauce-pans. In most cases it is possible to cook in the serving dishes. Vegetables may be strained after cooking and then returned to the cooking dish, which will remain hot by conduction, although dinner plates will have to be warmed by other means. Meat dishes which include sauces can nearly always be prepared, cooked and served in the same casserole. At the most one other dish will be required for preparing the food. Since many dishes can be cooked in the serving bowl which comes to the table, and some on the plate on which it is to be eaten, the washing-up chore is most satisfyingly reduced. Indeed food can be cooked in disposable paper containers if liked.

Should your family be quite incapable of cooking, they will at least be able to push a button, so prepare the breakfast the previous night and leave it in the refrigerator on individual plates. Write the heating time on a piece of paper and then cover the whole plate with plastic film. When the food is hot the family can discard the plastic film and paper and enjoy a hot and fresh breakfast.

The microwave oven has numerous advantages for the housewife and is a true release from a great deal of time-consuming labour. As the following recipes will show, it is invaluable for preparing meals quickly and for reheating a meal for a latecomer.

It has been mentioned previously that foods re-heat very quickly and this enables any member of the family to cook, and also enables the hostess to devote her individual attention to her dinner guests. Even when a pressure-cooker is used for last-minute vegetables it cannot be left unattended, since the timing is even more precise than in microwave cooking. Now vegetables can be pre-cooked (either conventionally or by microwave) and they will only require a moment's re-heating while the plates are brought to the table. Dishes of different foods may be re-heated in the oven at that same time and there will be no transference of flavour. After dinner coffee may be pre-percolated and the jug (not metal, of course) left in the oven, with the switch just ready to press.

Among the many advantages of the microwave oven speed comes high in the list. As cooking periods are so short, food often shows a great improvement in flavour and colour and retains a higher proportion of nutriment. Frozen peas which have been microwave-cooked properly can be mistaken for fresh peas. In fact the flavour actually improves. Shellfish, too, cooks admirably. The Japanese, whose sea-food cookery is so excellent, found that they could cook all their sea-food dishes in a microwave oven and did a great deal of important work in perfecting it.

Several hours can be saved in the thawing process of meat and poultry. A joint is ready for cooking 30 minutes after leaving the freezer. Frozen fruits should only be half-thawed, taking 2 minutes approximately.

For speedy last-minute cooking a jacket potato will be ready in 4 minutes and baked apples, stuffed as you wish, will take 1 minute for each apple. And when you have forgotten to buy bread, a large loaf from the freezer will be thawed for eating in 5 minutes.

The latest microwave ovens are equipped with an interrupt button which can be set to thaw for subsequent cooking. The timing mechanism switches itself on and off at set intervals. Future domestic ovens will have adjustable frequencies, some of which will be as low as 300 watts output. This will extend the range of microwave to dishes previously impossible to cook by this method, although the low wattage may slow the cooking rate down to the equivalent of a conventional oven.

Microwave cookery means freedom, cleanness and speed.

5

2 The Microwave Oven

There are two types of microwave ovens available at the moment, the catering and the domestic models. The power of the former is usually 2 kW, and the home kitchen type is usually 1 kW. The domestic microwave oven will cook only half as quickly, but this could be an advantage for it allows more room for permissible error in the timing. It does not matter if fish, meat or vegetables cook for one or two extra minutes, for only cakes, biscuits and egg dishes require exact timing. Larger ovens have only short timing mechanisms, but although some domestic types can be set for more than 30 minutes the food will not be harmed if the oven is switched off and the timer re-set. It is quite safe to switch off and open the door to test for cooking; cakes may sink but will revive and continue to cook when the current is turned on once again.

Most models look similar, consisting of a metal box, about 15in high x 22in wide x 17in to 18in deep, with inside measurements of approximately 9in x 14in x 13in. It is usually lined with stainless steel and equipped with a viewing panel of metal mesh, a shelf and an oven-light.

When choosing a cooker, be sure to purchase a model that has been approved. Safety regulations vary from country to country. At the time of writing, there are no British standards, but by the date of publication the BSI should have produced safety standards in conjunction with the Testing Laboratories of the Electricity Council. Check that service is likely to be prompt and that spare parts are available. Three-monthly technical inspections might be desirable.

As with other applicances improvements are taking place all the time and eventually there will be a model for domestic use incorporating a conventional oven, and metal dishes and containers will no longer be barred. A catering model made by Mealstream is on the market at the time of writing.

Home microwave ovens incorporating convection cooking or a browning element are now obtainable. These models are inevitably more expensive, but the cheaper and simpler microwave ovens are fine pieces of engineering equipment, simple to operate and highly satisfactory in the home.

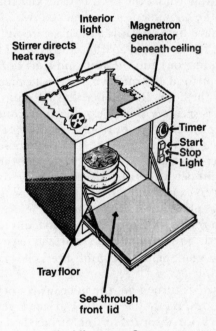

The Microwave Oven

The magnetron, which could be described as the heart of the oven, is situated in the top corner of the casing. This magnetron produces the microwaves which are distributed around the inside of the oven by a rotating fan. Microwaves travel in straight lines and will therefore bounce vertically and horizontally off the top, bottom and sides of the oven, through the food. The purpose of the shelf (tray floor) is to leave a space between the food and the oven base so that these waves can be reflected and thus reach all parts of what is being cooked.

The skill in designing the oven lies in arranging the fan and the magnetron so that the microwaves reach the food as evenly as possible, thereby achieving even and consistent cooking. In many of these recipes, the instructions require you to give the food a quarter turn at regular intervals. By doing this you are making doubly sure that the cooking will be even.

The operation of the oven is extemely simple. There is, of course, no heat control as in a conventional oven, and that means there is no waiting whilst the oven reaches the correct temperature. The whole of the cooking process depends entirely on timing.

The ovens have time controls and these are the only operational considerations for the cook, apart from the oven-light switch (to show what is going on) and the stop and start buttons.

To cook your food all you have to do is to place it on the base plate and lock the door. Remember that the oven will not operate until the door is securely shut. Turn the time control to the number you need and push the start button. This will not operate until the time control has been switched on. The time indicator will then revolve counter-clockwise back to zero and automatically switch off. Different models will have different timing devices and controls.

If you want to examine the food, to stir it or turn the dish during cooking, press the stop button and the oven-light will go out. When you replace the food in the oven and have shut the door, there is no need to re-set the timer, as it will have stopped automatically when you opened the door. Press the starter button and continue cooking.

When the oven is turned on, the microwaves penetrate the food from all directions. As they reach the surface layers they generate heat. Those rays not absorbed by the surface layers of food pass to the next layer and this process continues through to the centre. The penetration of the food is complete but the amount of energy absorbed by the succeeding layers declines, so that the temperature is not so high.

This loss of energy is noticeable after the first two or three inches of the outer layer of food. In contrast to cooking by external heat, however, the food is being cooked right through all the time, even though the outside is receiving more heat than the inside. Moreover, the inside is also receiving heat by ordinary conduction from the surrounding warm layers of food, as well as from the warm air in the oven, which has received its heat from the hot outer layers of food.

In this way the food can be cooked approximately uniformly and absolute uniformity can be achieved by allowing it to stand for a few seconds after it has been removed from the oven. The process of heat distribution throughout the food will continue for this brief period, the rate of distribution depending upon the type of food.

Scrambled eggs, for example, should be removed from the oven when just set and before they have reached the consistency usual when cooking on a conventional hob. Again, after a cooked roast or bird has been removed from the oven it should stand for a few moments to allow the residual heat in the outer part to reach the centre. This will happen more quickly with a chicken, which has a cavity in the middle, than with a solid roast. With a joint of beef the internal temperature will rise about $20°$ F for an average roast of $2\frac{1}{2}$ to 3 lb. For cuts of less than 2in, there is no difference in the time of cooking the outside and inner parts, for the microwaves penetrate this distance at their maximum intensity.

This means that it is difficult to brown a steak without drying it out and making it tough. The best plan is to cook it under a pre-heated grill long enough to seal both sides and then finish the cooking in the oven. In a 1 kW oven a 5-ounce fillet steak should take about 2 minutes.

The recipes and timing in this book were formulated using the Amana Radarange, which has similar power to other domestic models with an output of 650 watts. However, cooking times vary with each model and some are affected by the magnetron, so it is advisable to test a simple recipe on your own microwave oven and note how much faster or slower it cooks than the timing given in this book. You will then be able to allow for this when using the collection of recipes.

Running costs are much lower than those of a conventional oven because the cooking times are so much quicker.

The light bulb is more expensive than a normal one and so should be switched on only when it is necessary to view the cooking. Keep the machine switched off when not in use.

The magnetron is covered by a guarantee and has a long life. Its life is not of unlimited length and one day it will have to be replaced, like the cathode-ray tube in a television set.

To keep your microwave oven in pristine condition, remove and wash the base plate when soiled. The remainder of the oven only requires a wipe with a damp cloth and then a polish with a dry cloth.

Another method is to place a glass of hot water on the base plate and switch on the timer. When the water boils, the steam produced will coat the lining, which can be wiped dry. It is so easy to clean that bacon spatters or burst potatoes are of little concern. Never scrape off with a knife.

Always use oven gloves when removing containers from the oven, for although the dishes themselves do not cook they are heated by conduction from the food.

Do not rest dishes on the oven doors of the drop-down type. They are not strong enough and can become distorted, thus spoiling the seal.

Your microwave oven need not be sited in the kitchen. It could be placed on a side table in the dining or sitting room, and, provided it is not raining, even on the verandah or in the garden — anywhere in fact where there is a suitable electric socket. It can be taken to a week-end cottage or on a boat. A domestic model uses the usual 13-amp fused plug, but the larger and catering types will require a special "box" which your electrician will supply and fit.

As previously mentioned, you must re-think your cooking methods when you purchase a microwave oven. With the coming of the food-freezer thought had to be given to what would and what would not freeze, and to thawing times and bulk buying. The microwave will require an adjustment in cooking times and methods, but needs far less forward planning than conventional food preparation.

Start simply with a roast, giving less cooking time than stated. The meat cannot be spoilt, since the only fault could be under-cooking, and this can be rectified by putting the joint back in the oven for a further few minutes.

Each microwave oven is supplied with a small instruction book or leaflet. Usually some cooking times are given, but remember the very short times advertised are probably re-heating times and not cooking times. Cooking times depend on many factors, the wattage, the magnetron, the quantities in the oven at any particular time, the density and shape of the food and the water content. It will be noticed that different fats will melt at different rates, depending upon their composition.

If one item is cooked in one minute it does not follow that two items cooked at the same time will take 2 minutes and that three items will treble the time. A little time is saved on multiple cooking, for example if one item were to take $\frac{1}{2}$ minute to heat, two would take 50 seconds and four about 90 seconds. When cooking it is better to undertime and mixtures are more likely to be successful if they are too wet rather than too dry.

It also takes longer to heat or cook from the raw state two portions of food than one, because the number of microwaves in the oven is constant and with the presence of two items they have to do more work.

Microwaves penetrate food so rapidly that in order to produce a dish which is cooked consistently throughout the shape should be fairly uniform. A leg of lamb is an example of an unequally shaped piece of food, being thick at the thigh and narrow at the shin. The shin may become overcooked before the thigh end and to achieve a satisfactory roast it is better to bone the leg, and roll it and tie it into a compact shape before cooking. For the same reason, the legs and wings of a chicken should be well tucked into the body.

This aspect of microwave cookery must be borne in mind when preparing a complete meal on a plate for re-heating. Two very large potatoes, some very thinly sliced meat and a portion of peas will not heat up at the same rate and the result might be tepid potatoes, dried meat and shrivelled peas. It would be better to use smaller potatoes and thicker slices of meat. Alternatively if you are re-heating for several people, it is better to re-heat the items separately and reassemble them on to the plates.

Microwave cookery does not perform miracles of speed from basic ingredients and, of course, of itself it does not brown food, but the advantages will be realized after a very short period of ownership.

The latest cooking utensil available does permit food to be browned. It is a dish that makes frying in the microwave oven possible. Resembling a heat-proof glass casserole, it has a specially treated base which enables the dish to reach a temperature of 600°F. Fried eggs and bread, steaks, chops and the sealing of meats can be tackled successfully. The dish may be used with or without the lid depending on the crispness required.

One manufacturer is now producing a special mat and cover to bring about quick even thawing. The mat reduces edge heating and the cover focusses microwave heat into the centre of the frozen food. It is invaluable for thawing cooked soups and stews, which contain a high proportion of ice crystals.

Some models have a built-in grill for simultaneous use.

3 Containers and Cooking Equipment

No metal of any kind may be left in the oven during cooking. Dishes must be checked to make certain of this. Some new and exciting-looking coloured vitreous enamel cookware is in the shops and, while being highly desirable for conventional cooking, must not be used in the microwave oven, for the enamel is coating a base of cast iron.

Cups with metal or gold trim must also be avoided. When heating frozen foods remember to remove the foil containers.

If there is any metal present in the container it will reflect the microwaves instead of transmitting them and the food will not be cooked. This reflection also upsets the pattern of microwaves in the oven, causing "arc-ing", which may damage the magnetron.

Earthenware, wood, glass, paper, china, boil-in-the-bag bags (which are similar to the white bags that butchers use to wrap meat), roaster bags, plastic film, polypropylene and TPX are all suitable for use in the microwave oven.

Some plastics will develop holes very quickly and those unfortunately include the containers most readily available. Whether plastic ware can be used will depend upon its composition. Those suitable for freezing may be used for up to 30 minutes, before buckling.

Of the plastic materials mentioned, polypropylene is most easily recognizable. The pudding basins sometimes supplied with lids that are described as boilable are made of this substance. These bowls have a very long life and can be used frequently without much deterioration. Also available in similar material are rings which enable plates of food to be stacked and re-heated; 2 to 3 minutes is all that is necessary when re-heating vertically. With the rapidly developing demand this material will no doubt be manufactured in other shapes for all cooking purposes.

Plastic film, often described as self-clinging plastic film and recommended for wrapping sandwiches, is excellent when used to cover food cooking in a glass or earthenware dish. This material expands but does not explode. It is possible to see the food during cooking and the plastic film prevents moisture from escaping. Plastic film can also be used for lining cake dishes. There is no need to puncture this film. The other types of bags mentioned must either be punctured or tied loosely, otherwise they will burst. Do not use the metal tags supplied with these bags.

Greaseproof paper may be used either as an oven lining or as a cover where a seal is not required.

Vegetable parchment because of its non-stick properties may be used to line cake dishes. This saves the chore of greasing and lining.

Kitchen paper is absorbent and useful for preparing fatty foods, such as bacon, sausages, pork chops, etc. Use it to line the base of the dish and as a cover.

The wide range of permissible cooking materials should allow you to make use of many containers already in your possession, but you must decide whether you prefer to invest in long-lasting dishes, such as toughened glass and earthenware, or to use disposables.

If in doubt whether a plate or dish is strong enough for microwave use, stand a half-filled glass of water on it. Place in the oven and heat for one minute. The water should be warm but the platter cool or only slightly warm at the edge. If it is hotter than the water it would be unwise to use it.

Pots should be large enough to allow for not boiling over. This is particularly important when cooking sauces containing milk or boiling syrup, or jam where a continuous rolling boil is required.

Regardless of any future improvements in the microwave oven and the production of other suitable cooking materials, the recipes in this book will remain applicable.

4 The Cooking Process

The recipes in this book have been written and set out in a special way. This should make it considerably easier to follow the directions for this new medium of cooking. The steps have been written down numerically, so that you can see where you are at any point. The cooking times for each step have been printed at the right-hand side of the page. By adding these the total cooking time for each recipe can be calculated. Preparation for the next stage can be in hand whilst the microwave oven is cooking the previously prepared one and this will speed up the production line. It is recommended that when preparing food from one of these recipes all the ingredients are weighed out first and left on a tray ready to be used. Remember that microwave cookery allows for interruptions and generally food will not be spoiled if only half the recipe is completed at one specific time.

When turning the dish while cooking or stirring always remove the spoon before restarting the cooking process. In some cases you are advised to cook the food covered or uncovered. This is not of paramount importance, but if you wish to crispen or brown it is better to leave the dish uncovered. For hastening cooking time the cover should be left on to keep heat and moisture enclosed.

Foods which cook well in the microwave oven include white meats, poultry and all types of fish and shellfish. Most vegetables will cook from the raw state in small quantities. Chops and steaks, which are not included in the recipes, can be cooked in a few minutes, but if you prefer them brown they must be sealed under a hot grill first. Alternatively they can be covered with a sauce. Cakes, particularly those with a high fat and syrup content, are successful. Chocolate or dark mixtures will not need to be iced. Light yeast sponge mixtures respond well and are quick to cook. Rice and pastas cook and re-heat splendidly.

The microwave oven will crispen, but will not fry normally. Onions will fry if given sufficient time and joints of chicken will brown because of the long cooking time. Chipped and roast potatoes may be re-heated, but not cooked from their raw state in the oven.

The oven cannot perform the miracle of tenderizing tough meat. Overcome this factor by using good-quality meat, cut into small pieces. A tenderizer is a useful implement for batting and softening the tissues. Powdered tenderizers made from the juice of the papaya may be sprinkled on to the surface of the meat, or a marinade can be prepared and utilized.

Foods which cannot be cooked by microwave include Yorkshire pudding, soufflés, meringues, éclairs and cream buns. Puff or flaky pastry will not be successful but any pastry which does not need to rise may be cooked in the oven. However, the results cannot be the same as with pastry conventionally cooked. It is better to cook large quantities of vegetables in the pressure-cooker and serve immediately or leave for re-heating in the oven.

The microwave oven will re-heat any pre-cooked foods by whatever method they have been prepared. Items such as fish and vegetables can be cooked from the frozen state and re-heated or pre-cooked, and frozen dishes cut the freezer-to-table time by 75 per cent.

The food-freezer, microwave oven and conventional cooker all play their part in producing good fare. Defrost raw steak in the oven and then grill conventionally. Pre-fried eggs are easily re-heated and the yolk will not harden, provided that in the initial cooking it has been lightly basted with some of the cooking fat. Poached eggs and omelettes will also re-heat satisfactorily.

Primary cooking can be carried out in the microwave oven and the food then frozen in suitable portions for subsequent re-heating. Cooking in small quantities by the medium of microwave adds variety and freshness to the diet. Small quantities of jam are easily prepared, as are pastas and pâtés, and even a Christmas cake can be ready in a few hours. Do not overcook foods which are to be re-heated later, or on re-heating they will be too soft. Sauces tend to thicken when cold but this can always be rectified by adding a little more liquid when re-heating.

Although no recipes are specifically given for preparing food for the freezer, some may be found suitable. However, any foods prepared from recipes from a freezer cookery book may be thawed or cooked by microwave.

Accelerated freeze-dried (AFD) foods can be re-constituted and cooked by microwave. They may be mixed with cold water, but it may be found quicker to use a kettle and add the water hot, for a good electric kettle will boil in 2 minutes the same amount of water as the microwave will boil in 4 to 6 minutes.

Every recipe in this book has been tested and eaten by my family. I would particularly like to thank Dilys for her able assistance. Even if you do not possess a microwave oven I hope you will enjoy browsing through this book. All the recipes can be cooked conventionally. Do not be afraid to use your own ideas. Experiment with roasting coffee beans, chestnuts, etc., and I am sure that you will find cooking a pleasant pastime, rather than a boring chore.

Before turning to the recipes make yourself a cup of "Instant" coffee: $\frac{1}{2}$ cup of water, $\frac{1}{4}$ cup of milk and 1 tsp "Instant" coffee. $1\frac{1}{2}$ minutes in the oven, piping hot to drink and no saucepan to wash up.

5 Weights and Measures

For culinary purposes it is not practicable to convert pounds and ounces accurately into kilogrammes. In some recent cookery books you will see, for example, ¼ lb (112 g). This is almost exactly correct, but rather useless to a cook with scales whose smallest divisions are likely to be 25 grammes, or with a set of weights having 5 grammes as the smallest unit. In this book the smallest quantity given in the recipes is 10 grammes. An ounce is 28·35 grammes so that a few grammes will be the weight of a pinch of salt and will make little difference to the completed recipe.

Conversion from ounces to grammes is difficult, as the value of an ounce lies between 25 grammes and 30 grammes, but is substantially nearer the latter. Whilst it is accepted that 25 grammes is likely to be the basic minimum weight in cookery books written in the future, I have adopted a 30-gramme conversion in the recipes. This will mean that you can continue to use the proportions you are used to and those without metric scales or weights can continue to use their avoirdupois ones. In other words, this is a book written by a housewife to enable other housewives to do their best in a changing period, in easily understood terms, for I am sure it will be quite a time before we lose the habit of thinking in ounces and pints. Similarly I have used fractions in some places instead of decimals, although this is not in accordance with the advice given by the Metrication Board. A useful leaflet called "Going Metric: Everyday Units" can be obtained from them at News Room, 22 Kingsway, London WC2.

The metric equivalents used in this book are therefore as follows (adjustments being made in the larger quantities to allow for the fact that an ounce is in fact slightly less than 30 grammes):

Ounces	Grammes
$\frac{1}{4}$	10
$\frac{1}{2}$	15
$\frac{3}{4}$	20
1	30
$1\frac{1}{2}$	45
2	60
3	90
4	110
5	140
6	170
7	200
8	230
12	340
1 pound	450
$1\frac{1}{2}$ lb	680
$2-2\frac{1}{2}$ lb	1 kilogramme

Liquid Measure

1 litre equals $1\frac{3}{4}$ British pints. The British pint consists of 20 imperial fluid ounces. This composite table gives close equivalents for working purposes.

Pints	Fluid Ounces	Litres	Millilitres (ml)
2	40	1·15	1150
$1\frac{3}{4}$	35	1	1000
$1\frac{1}{2}$	30	0·85	850
$1\frac{1}{4}$	25	0·7	700
1	20	0·55	550
$\frac{3}{4}$	15	0·4	425
$\frac{1}{2}$	10	0·3	300
$\frac{1}{4}$ (1 gill)	5	0·15	150
$\frac{1}{8}$	$2\frac{1}{2}$	0·07	70

On the Continent liquid measure is often in litres and decilitres (dl). the decilitre being 0·1 litre and equal to $3\frac{1}{2}$ fluid ounces. However, for simplicity, in this book the liquid measure conversion has been based on 2 pints to the litre.

American equivalents are not printed in the recipes but the following will help you to convert:
1·75 Imperial pints = 1 litre = 2·094 American pints.
To obtain Imperial pints, multiply American pints by 0·84
To obtain American pints, multiply Imperial pints by 1·2.
Solid measurements are identical but

1 American pint = 16 fluid ounces
1 Imperial pint = 20 fluid ounces
$\frac{1}{2}$ Imperial pint = $1\frac{1}{4}$ American cups
$\frac{2}{5}$ Imperial pint = 1 American cup

Linear Measurements

Inches	Centimetres (cm)	Millimetres (mm)
1	$2\frac{1}{2}$	25
2	$5\frac{1}{2}$	50
6	$15\frac{1}{2}$	150
7	18	175
9	23	225
10	$25\frac{1}{2}$	250

6 Abbreviations and Terms used in this Book

tbsp   = tablespoon(s)
tsp   = teaspoon(s)
oz   = ounce(s)
pt   = pint(s)
lit   = litre(s)
g   = gramme(s)
kg   = kilogramme(s)
Oven   = Microwave oven
Hob   = Electric boiling ring or gas ring
Conventional   = Using electric, gas or solid-fuel cooker
Suitable dish   = Casserole, or serving dish of a suitable size and material for use in the microwave oven, i.e. without any metal content.
Stir   = Open the oven, remove the cooking dish and stir, making sure all the food is moved around.
Blend   = Mix well with a spatula or back of a spoon to press out any lumps.
Cook . . . minutes = Total cooking time unless other instructions are given.
Turning = Turning the entire dish within the oven without removing the dish.
$\frac{1}{4}$ turn   = Turn dish through 90 degrees.
$\frac{1}{2}$ turn   = Turn dish through 180 degrees.

7 Soups

Two basic methods for making soups are those where vegetables are cooked, puréed and blended in a white sauce and unthickened soups where small pieces of vegetables are suspended in a good stock.

A good variety of methods of making soups is shown here.

Cucumber and spinach soups are based on a white sauce.

A suitable soup for figure-watchers is carrot soup, where the cooked vegetables are suspended in stock.

Kidney soup is thickened in the final stages with a solution of flour and water, and pea soup with cornflour.

Croûtons are small squares of dried bread traditionally fried in hot fat or toasted, but are just as good cooked by microwave. Croûtons should be re-heated and dropped into the hot soup at the moment of serving.

You will recognize the puff balls as choux pastry mixture. When you are making éclairs or profiteroles in your conventional oven, scrape the surplus mixture from the sides of the bowl and use for making puff balls in the microwave oven. If the mixture is prepared specially for these savouries a large quantity will be produced and they will keep perfectly for several weeks.

Carrot Health Soup

$\frac{1}{2}$ lb (230 g) carrots
1 beef stock cube ⎫
1 pt ($\frac{1}{2}$ lit) water ⎬ or 1 pt ($\frac{1}{2}$ lit) stock
$\frac{1}{2}$ oz (15 g) butter

Juice of $\frac{1}{2}$ orange
1 tbsp chopped fresh parsley
Salt, pepper

1   Peel or scrape carrots. Grate on coarse grater.

2 Melt butter in suitable bowl in microwave oven.   *Cook 30 seconds.*

3 Toss carrots in butter and add ¼ pt (⅛ lit) water or stock.
Cover.

Cook 3 minutes, stirring after 1½ minutes.

4 Add stock cube, salt, pepper, and parsley (not too much salt).

Cook 5 minutes. Stir.

5 Add remainder of water and orange juice.   *Cook 4 minutes.*

6 Adjust seasoning if necessary.

Cucumber Soup

1 large cucumber
1 pt (½ lit) stock or 1 pt (½ lit) water and 1 chicken stock cube.
½ oz (15 g) butter
½ oz (15 g) flour
⅛ pt (70 ml) milk
⅛ pt (70 ml) cream
Salt, pepper

1 Wash cucumber. Skin. Cut in half lengthwise and remove pips.

2 Cut cucumber into tiny dice and drop into boiling salted water, bring back to boil. Strain.

3 Place butter in a large suitable casserole to melt.   *Cook ½ minute.*

4 Stir in flour.   *Cook ½ minute.*

5 Add stock or water and stock cube and seasoning. Add cucumber.   *Cook 10 minutes.*

6 Liquidize or put through a mouli-légumes or sieve.

7 Stir in milk and re-heat.   *Cook 2 minutes approximately.*

8 Add cream. Adjust seasoning.

If desired reserve a few dice of cucumber before liquidizing and return to soup before serving.

Kidney Soup

½ lb (230 g) ox kidney   1 onion
1 pt (½ lit) water or stock   1 carrot

1 small turnip	Salt, pepper
2 mushrooms	$\frac{1}{2}$ oz (15 g) flour
1 stick of celery	$\frac{1}{2}$ oz (15 g) margarine
Bouquet garni	1 tbsp sweet sherry
Lemon juice	

1 Melt fat in suitable large casserole.	*Cook 20 seconds.*
2 Peel vegetables and chop finely.	
3 Add vegetables to fat. Stir.	*Cook 7 minutes stirring once or twice during cooking.*
4 Wash kidney in cold salted water and remove membrane and core.	
5 Chop kidney very finely.	
6 Add kidney, lemon juice, bouquet garni, salt, pepper, and water or stock to vegetables.	*Cook uncovered for 15 minutes.*
7 Remove bouquet garni and liquidize or put through a sieve or a mouli-légumes.	
8 Blend flour with a little cold water and add to soup.	
9 Replace in oven and bring to boil to thicken.	*Cook 3 minutes.*
10 Stir in sherry. Taste and correct seasoning.	
11 Serve hot.	

French Onion Soup

$\frac{1}{2}$ lb (230 g) best quality Spanish onions
2 oz (60 g) butter
1 beef stock cube
$\frac{1}{8}$ pt (70 ml) red wine
1 pt ($\frac{1}{2}$ lit) water
Salt, pepper
4 thick slices of toast from a French loaf
Grated cheese

1 Peel onions and slice thinly.	
2 Place butter in a suitable dish and melt.	*Cook 1 minute.*
3 Mix onions into butter.	*Cook 10 minutes, stirring every $2\frac{1}{2}$ minutes.*
4 Add stock cube, wine, water and seasoning	*Cook 12 minutes, stirring every 4 minutes.*
5 Place toast in base of soup dish. Pour soup over and sprinkle with grated cheese.	

6   Flash under a hot grill so that the cheese is
    just melted.

This traditional soup, known in France as Soupe à l'oignon gratinée,
can be a meal in itself.

Pea Soup

12 oz (340 g) fresh or frozen peas
$\frac{1}{2}$ oz (15 g) butter
$\frac{1}{4}$ level tsp celery salt
1 small onion
1 pt ($\frac{1}{2}$ lit) chicken stock or 1 pt ($\frac{1}{2}$ lit) water and 1 chicken stock cube
Salt, pepper
Sprig of fresh mint
2 tsp cornflour
2 tbsp single cream

1 Melt butter in suitable casserole.	*Cook $\frac{1}{2}$ minute.*
2 Chop onion finely and add. Stir.	*Cook 2 minutes.*
3 Add peas, salt, pepper, celery salt and mint.	
4 Bring stock to boil on conventional hob.	
5 Add stock to peas, replace casserole in oven.	*Cook 6 minutes.*
6 Remove mint and liquidize soup. Press through a sieve.	
7 Blend cornflour with 1 tbsp cold water and stir into soup. Return soup to oven to bring to the boil.	*Cook 3 minutes approximately.*
8 Correct seasoning. Stir in cream and serve hot, or chill and stir in cream just before serving.	

For a variation add a little chopped ham to the hot soup. Ham is an
excellent flavouring for peas.

Cream of Spinach Soup

1 large packet frozen chopped spinach
$1\frac{1}{2}$ oz (45 g) butter
$1\frac{1}{2}$ oz (45 g) cornflour
1 pt ($\frac{1}{2}$ lit) milk

Salt, pepper
$\frac{1}{4}$ tsp nutmeg
Squeeze of garlic powder
1 tbsp sour cream

1 Blend cornflour with a little of the cold milk in a large suitable casserole.
2 Add remainder of milk and stir well.
3 Add the butter, nutmeg and garlic powder.

Cook 4 minutes stirring every $\frac{1}{2}$ minute to break up any possible lumps.

4 Remove casserole from oven and whisk the sauce with a balloon or loop whisk. Season.

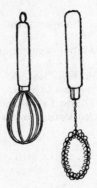

Whisks (*left*, balloon whisk; *right*, loop whisk)

5 Place spinach either frozen or thawed in sauce.

Cook 4 to 10 minutes depending upon the solidity of the spinach. Stir occasionally.

6 When the spinach is blended and the soup is very hot remove from oven and press through a sieve.
7 Taste and adjust seasoning.
8 Before serving re-heat in the oven.
9 Remove from oven and add the sour cream.

The sour cream greatly improves the flavour and texture of this soup and turns it from being a simple spinach soup into superb crème.

Serves 4.

Tomato Soup

$\frac{1}{2}$ oz (15 g) butter
$\frac{1}{2}$ oz (15 g) flour
1 onion, chopped
1 lb (450 g) tomatoes or 15 oz (430 g) can of tomatoes

Bouquet garni	1 chicken stock cube
Salt, pepper	1 tsp Worcestershire sauce
1¼ pt (370 ml) water	Squeeze of lemon juice

1 Place butter and chopped onion in a casserole. *Cook 2 minutes.*
2 Add flour and seasoning. *Cook 1 minute, stir*
3 Add tomatoes, roughly chopped, bouquet garni,
   ½ pt (¼ lit) water and the stock cube. Cover. *Cook 5 minutes,
   stirring every 2
   minutes.*

4 Remove from oven. Remove bouquet garni
   but reserve.
5 Liquidize or pass through a mouli-légumes or
   sieve.
6 Thin down soup with remainder of water.
7 Add Worcestershire sauce and lemon juice.
8 Adjust seasoning. Replace bouquet garni and
   bring to boil either on conventional hob or in
   oven. *Cook 5 minutes.*

If you use canned tomatoes, make sure that the quantity of liquid
is not exceeded.

Watercress Soup

2 bunches watercress
1 oz (30 g) butter
1 oz (30 g) flour
1 pt (½ lit) milk
Salt, pepper
Additional milk or water

1 Wash watercress thoroughly in cold water and
   remove most of the thick stalks.
2 Place ½ pt (¼ lit) water in suitable container and
   put in oven and bring to boil. *4 minutes.*
3 Mix watercress with water, cover with paper
   and bring to boil. *3 minutes.*
4 Remove from oven and drain.
5 Prepare sauce: (*a*) **Melt** butter in large container. *½ minute.*
   (*b*) Stir in flour. *Cook ½ minute.*
   (*c*) Add milk gradually,
   blending well.
6 Add watercress and cook to thicken. *3 minutes stirring
   every ½ minute.*

7 Continue cooking for: *2 minutes.*
8 Remove from oven and liquidize or pass
   through a sieve or mouli-légumes.
9 Make up to 1¼ pt (700 ml) with milk or water,
   return to oven.   *3 minutes.*
10 Season to taste.

Watercress soup has a delicate flavour and provides a good supply
of iron to the diet.

Quick Croûtons

3 ¼ in-thick slices of white bread
2 oz (60 g) butter

1 Remove crusts from bread.
2 Cut each slice into ½ in squares.
3 Line oven-sheet with greaseproof paper.
4 Spread bread cubes on paper.   *Cook 1 minute.*
5 Lift sides of paper and shake croûtons.   *Cook 1 minute.*
   Repeat this process until the croûtons are hard
   but not coloured. Approximately twice more.
6 Remove from oven.
7 Melt butter in large suitable dish in oven.   *Cook 1½ minutes.*
8 Toss croûtons in the butter immediately

Croûtons will keep several days in a screwtopped jar or plastic
container in a refrigerator.
   This quantity is sufficient for 6 servings, dropped into hot
soups.

Soup Puffballs

1½ oz (45 g) plain flour   1 standard egg
1 oz (30 g) soft margarine   Pinch of salt
⅛ pt (70 ml) water

1 Place water in suitable glass jug with salt and
   margarine.   *Cook 1½ minutes*
                                                       to boil.
2 When liquid is boiling fast, remove from oven
   and toss flour in. Stir vigorously.

3 Leave to cool a few minutes.
4 Add egg and beat thoroughly until the mixture
   is thick and shiny.
5 Transfer mixture to a forcing bag and using a
   $\frac{1}{2}$ in plain nozzle, pipe 50 tiny dots on to a piece
   of greaseproof paper.
6 Place paper on oven glass base.   *Cook 7 minutes,*
                                                  turning paper $\frac{1}{4}$ turn
                                                  every minute.

 These can be stored in a screwtop jar in a refrigerator for several
weeks.
   Drop a few into hot soup just before serving.
   For a variation add 1 oz (30 g) grated cheese to mixture after the
egg is incorporated.
   A tip for adding the flour is to weigh it out on greaseproof paper.
This enables you to toss the flour into the jug quickly with no
spillage.

8　Fish Dishes

Perhaps the microwave oven gives its best performance when cooking fish. The fish retains its juices and therefore the flavour is improved, and for those on salt-free diets it is more palatable. Any white fish may be cooked whole or filleted. Try a Dover sole, sprinkled with salt and coarsely ground pepper, dab with butter, cover with plastic film and cook for 3 minutes. Provided your oven is large enough, whole freshwater fish may be cooked. Salmon trout should be treated in the same way as cold salmon, but of course extra cooking time must be allowed. All shellfish re-heat well and scampi, shrimps, prawns, crawfish and lobster may all be used in microwave dishes. Mackerel should be treated as herring. Ring the changes when cooking haddock or cod by using different sauces. It is possible to prepare a sauce in a suitable casserole and then add the fish fillets to cook for 3 to 4 extra minutes.

Canned fish such as pilchards, salmon and tuna may be re-heated in the oven with mashed potato or cooked spaghetti for a quick supper dish.

Smoked haddock and cod need no extra moisture, butter is optional, but if used the dish must be well sealed with plastic film.

If you enjoy eating fish, whether fresh or frozen, you will prefer to have it cooked by microwaves.

Baked Stuffed Herrings

2 fresh medium-sized herrings	1 tsp salt
1 tsp lemon juice	Pepper

Stuffing

3 oz (90 g) sliced mushrooms	1 tbsp grated onion

½ tsp lemon juice
½ oz (15 g) butter
Salt, pepper

1 tbsp chopped parsley (fresh)
2 sheets baking parchment

1   Fillet herrings by opening down the front and
pressing on the backbone with knuckles.

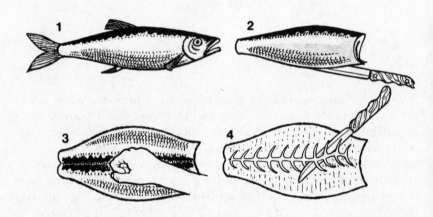

Filleting herrings

1   Herring on its side.   2   Slit along underside of fish.   3   Press along
shiny outside of fish, having opened it up along spine.   4   Turn fish over
and lift out spine, using blunt edge of knife.

2   Rub lemon juice into inside of fish. Season.
Leave aside.
3   Mix mushrooms with onion and butter. Cover.   *Cook 2 minutes.*
4   Add lemon juice, seasoning and parsley.
5   Open herrings on to parchment. Spread half of
stuffing on each and fold to original shape.
6   Wrap each fish in parchment. Seal well.
7   Place on dish or plate.   *Cook 3 minutes for
each fish, 6 minutes
if cooking together,
turning plate once.*

8   To serve, gently remove parchment and slide
fish on to a plate.

Economical and nutritious. Herrings contain a liberal amount
of Vitamin D.

Soused Herrings

2 herrings   Vinegar
1 medium-sized onion   Mace
Salt, pepper   Peppercorns

1 Fillet herrings.
2 Season and roll up.
3 Slice onions and place in bottom of dish.
4 Place herrings on bed of onions.
5 Add 3 crushed peppercorns and blade of mace.
6 Mix equal quantities of vinegar and water so
   that the liquid reaches half way up the herrings.
7 Leave 1 hour to marinate, basting frequently.
8 Cover with greaseproof paper.

*Cook 6 minutes,
turning dish ½ turn
after 3 minutes.*

Poached Salmon

2 4-oz (110-g) steaks of fresh salmon   Lemon juice
1 oz (30 g) butter   Salt, pepper

1 Place salmon steaks in a suitable serving dish.
2 Dot with butter, season and add a squeeze of
   lemon juice.
3 Cover with plastic film.

*Cook 6 minutes
approximately,
turning dish ¼ turn
every 2 minutes.*

4 Test to see if salmon is cooked.

Use this recipe for frozen salmon but cook 2 minutes, turning
dish a ½ turn after 1 minute, and then leave in oven for 20 minutes
before completing cooking. This is to allow the fish to thaw
completely, to avoid toughening.

Cold Salmon

4 4-oz (110-g) cutlets of fresh or frozen salmon
1 pt (½ lit) water
1 tbsp malt vinegar
1 onion, thinly sliced
1 small carrot, thinly sliced   Bayleaf
                                             Salt, pepper

1 Place water, vinegar, onion, carrot, bayleaf and seasoning in a suitable casserole.	*Cook 5 minutes*
2 Wash salmon in cold water, removing any blood clots with salt. Rinse.	
3 Place salmon in liquor and baste.	*Cook 5 minutes, test.*
4 Remove casserole from oven and leave salmon to cool in the liquor.	
5 Before serving remove salmon from liquor and place on a bed of lettuce.	

The liquor is called a Court Bouillon and may be used to cook any white fish or freshwater fish, when it will impart a very delicate flavour.

When the fish is cooked the skin and bones should easily come away from the flesh when separated with a fork.

Remember the salmon will continue to cook as the liquor cools.

Salmon Chauffage

15 oz (425 g) can of salmon (good-quality pink is satisfactory).
$\frac{1}{2}$ lb (230 g) cooked peas
1 small onion
2 tbsp chopped fresh parsley
3 oz (90 g) butter or margarine
3 oz (90 g) flour
1 pt ($\frac{1}{2}$ lit) milk
Salt, pepper
1 oz (30 g) butter or margarine ⎫ Topping
2 oz (60 g) fresh breadcrumbs ⎭

1 Melt butter in suitable casserole.	*Cook 1½ minutes,*
2 Chop onion finely and add.	*Cook 2 minutes.*
3 Stir in flour and blend. Add milk. Stir.	*Cook to thicken 4 minutes. Stir every minute.*
4 Remove large bones and skin from salmon and add to sauce with peas and parsley.	
5 Season to taste.	*Cook to re-heat 3 minutes.*
6 Fry breadcrumbs on conventional hob in 1 oz (30 g) butter until golden.	
7 Sprinkle crumbs over salmon and serve hot.	

Fresh salmon, which is at its cheapest in June and July, may be used instead of the canned variety to turn this into a luxury dish. Garnish with asparagus tips.

Salmon Salad Mould

½ lb (230 g) can of salmon
½ oz (15 g) (1 packet) gelatine
3 tbsp water
1½ oz (45 g) butter
1½ oz (45 g) flour
½ pt (¼ lit) milk
1 tbsp salad cream
Dash Worcestershire sauce
Salt, pepper
Peas, diced cucumber, skinned and diced tomato = 2 tbsp approx.
Sliced cucumber for garnish.

1 Open can of salmon, drain, remove large bones
   and black skin. Mash well.
2 Place gelatine in water. Stir. Place in oven.   *Cook 20 seconds.*
   Stir. Leave to clear.
3 Blend flour with cold milk, in medium-sized
   glass mixing bowl. Add butter.   *Cook 3 minutes,
                                                    stirring every ½
                                                    minute.*
4 Beat well with wooden spoon.
5 When gelatine and sauce mixture are of equal
   temperatures, add gelatine to sauce.
6 Add other ingredients and mix well. Taste.
7 Turn into ring mould and refrigerate for 2
   hours.
8 Turn out. Garnish with cucumber slices.
   Serve with a green salad.

When adding gelatine to mixtures, the temperatures should be
similar to avoid roping. Always pour dissolved gelatine from a
height. This will help to cool the gelatine when mixing.

Macédoine of Fish

1 lb (450 g) fish (cod or haddock fillet)   ½ pt (¼ lit) mayonnaise
½ oz (15 g) butter   4 slices of tomato
2 oz (60 g) cooked peas   4 slices of hard-boiled egg
2 carrots, cooked and sliced   Salt, pepper

4 scallop shells

1 Skin fish and cut into 1-in squares.

2 Place fish in suitable dish. Dot with butter.
Season with pepper and salt. Cover with greaseproof paper.

Cook 6 minutes,
turning dish every
1½ minutes.

3 Allow to cool.
4 Mix carrots and peas together and divide
between 4 shells.
5 Cover vegetables with fish.
6 Spread mayonnaise over fish and garnish with
the slices of tomato and egg.

This is an excellent hors-d'œuvre or summer supper dish, served
with a green salad.

Haddock Fillets Pomadoro

1 lb (450 g) fresh haddock fillet
1 oz (30 g) butter or margarine
1 oz (30 g) flour
½ pt (¼ lit) milk
15 oz (430 g) can of tomatoes
½ level tsp dried tarragon
Salt, pepper

1 Skin haddock fillets and place in a suitable
casserole. Season. Cover.

Cook 4 minutes, turn
dish ½ turn after 2
minutes.

2 Place butter in suitable bowl in oven.   *Cook ½ minute.*
3 Add flour and blend.   *Cook ½ minute.*
4 Add milk gradually.

Cook 3 minutes,
stirring every
minute.

5 Thin down the sauce with liquor from the
tomatoes. Stir well. Add tarragon and seasoning.
6 Pour sauce over fish and cover with tomatoes.
Cover dish with plastic film.

Cook 3 minutes; turn
dish ¼ turn every
minute.

7 Taste sauce before serving and adjust seasoning
if necessary.

Garnish with fleurons of puff pastry and serve with boiled
potatoes or runner beans.

To skin fillets of white fish: lay skin-down on a board. Dip the fingers of one hand in salt and hold the tail firmly on the edge of the board. Using a very sharp knife lift the flesh from the skin at the tail, starting at the tail end. Hold the knife at a very slight angle and push the centre of the blade towards the top of the fish between skin and flesh.

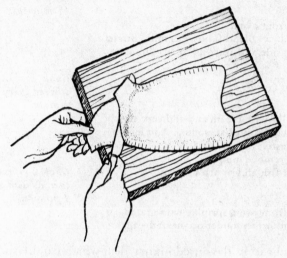

Skinning white-fish fillets

Fillets of Fish in Egg, Cream and Wine Sauce

1 lb (450 g) fillets of fish (haddock, cod, halibut), skinned
1 tbsp chopped spring onions
Salt, pepper
$\frac{1}{4}$ oz (10 g) butter
$\frac{1}{4}$ pt (150 ml) dry white wine
$\frac{1}{4}$ pt (150 ml) water

Sauce

1½ oz (45 g) butter	2 egg yolks
1½ oz (45 g) flour	$\frac{1}{4}$ pt (150 ml) cream
$\frac{1}{4}$ pt (150 ml) milk	Lemon juice
$\frac{1}{8}$ pt ($\frac{1}{4}$ lit) fish liquor	1 to 2 tbsp grated cheese

1   Place half the onions in base of suitable casserole.

2 Season fish fillets and place on top.
3 Add remainder of onion.
4 Cover with wine and water mixed.
5 Cover with greased greaseproof paper and set
  aside for as long as possible ($\frac{1}{2}$ hour to 2 hours).
6 Place dots of butter on fish, replace greased
  greaseproof paper.

Cook 5 minutes,
turning dish every
$1\frac{1}{2}$ minutes.

7 Remove from oven.
8 Prepare sauce. Blend flour with milk. Strain
  fish, put aside and add $\frac{1}{2}$ pt ($\frac{1}{4}$ lit) liquor to
  sauce.
9 Add butter.

Cook 4 minutes,
stirring every $\frac{1}{2}$
minute.

10 Blend yolks with cream and add very slowly
   to hot sauce. Adjust seasoning. Add lemon
   juice to taste.
11 Strain to remove lumps.
12 Pour over fish and return to oven.

Cook 2 minutes,
turning dish after
1 minute.

13 Remove from oven, sprinkle with grated
   cheese and brown under pre-heated grill.

This is a delicately flavoured luxury dish which can be successfully
re-heated for dinner parties.

Sole Céri

2 skinned and filleted sole (cut into 8 fillets)
Salt, pepper
$\frac{1}{4}$ pt (150 ml) dry white wine
Bayleaf
$\frac{1}{2}$ oz (15 g) butter
$\frac{1}{2}$ oz (15 g) flour
2 oz (60 g) prawns
2 tbsp single cream
2 oz (60 g) peeled and stoned grapes for garnish
Fish stock
Fish bones and skin
1 small onion
Parsley stalks (optional)
Juice of $\frac{1}{2}$ lemon
Salt, pepper
Water

1 Prepare the fish stock on a conventional hob. Place all ingredients in a saucepan and just cover with water.
2 Bring to boil and simmer no more than 15 minutes (over-simmering causes the stock to become bitter).
3 Strain into jug and set aside.
4 Sprinkle fillets with salt and pepper and roll up top to tail.
5 Place in a suitable dish.

Sole Céri

6 Add half the wine, bayleaf and enough fish stock to cover. Cover with greaseproof paper.

Cook 5 minutes, turn dish $\frac{1}{2}$ turn after 2 minutes.

Test fish to make sure it is cooked.
7 Remove fish from sauce and keep hot.
8 Add remainder of wine to sauce.

Cook 2 minutes.

9 Blend flour and butter together in a small bowl, using a teaspoon.
10 Beat flour and butter mixture into sauce, a little at a time.

Cook 3 minutes stirring every minute.

11 Add prawns.

Cook 2 minutes.

12 Season and add cream.
13 Pour sauce over and around fish and garnish with grapes.

The sauce should be the consistency of cream. When sole is expensive use plaice — the result will be almost as good.
    Serve with broccoli and creamed potatoes.

Sole Mornay (Fillets of lemon sole in cheese sauce)

4 fillets of lemon sole
lemon juice
salt, pepper
$\frac{1}{4}$ oz (10 g) butter

Sauce

1 oz (30 g) butter
1 oz (30 g) flour
$\frac{1}{2}$ pt ($\frac{1}{4}$ lit) milk
2 oz (60 g) grated hard cheese
Bayleaf
$\frac{1}{2}$ onion, thinly sliced
salt, pepper

1 Heat but do not boil milk in suitable jug in oven with onion and bayleaf. Set aside.	*2 minutes.*
2 Wash fish in cold water, remove excess moisture. Skin if desired.	
3 Sprinkle fillets with lemon juice, season and roll up head to tail. Dot with butter.	
4 Place fish in suitable dish that just fits and cook covered with greaseproof paper.	*6 minutes; turn dish $\frac{1}{2}$ turn after 3 minutes.*
5 Remove casserole and set aside.	
6 Strain the milk to remove onion and bayleaf.	
7 Melt butter in suitable basin in oven $\frac{1}{2}$ minute.	
8 Blend in flour.	*Cook $\frac{1}{2}$ minute.*
9 Add milk and stir well.	*Cook 3 minutes. Stir every minute.*
10 Remove surplus juices from fish and add to sauce.	
11 Add cheese. Taste. Correct seasoning.	
12 Pour sauce over fish.	*Cook 2 minutes to re-heat.*

Two or three prawns rolled inside the fillets will enhance this dish which could be served as a second course in a four-course dinner or as a light supper dish.

Garnish with puff pastry fleurons. To make these roll left-over pieces of puff pastry to the thickness of a 5p piece. Cut into small crescent shapes using an upturned egg-cup as a guide. Bake in a pre-heated conventional oven 425°F (218°C) for 8 to 10 minutes until risen and crisp.

Store in airtight container.

These may be re-heated to refresh.

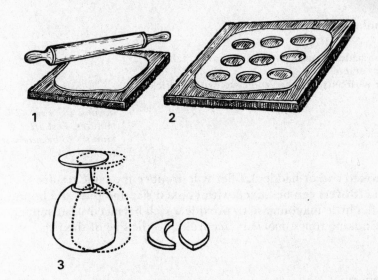

Cutting pastry fleurons or crescents

1 Roll out pastry. 2 Cut circles with egg-cup. 3 On each circle move egg-cup $\frac{1}{4}$ in away from one edge; press and remove to leave a crescent shape.

Buttered Fillets of Plaice

Fillets of plaice
Salt, pepper
Lemon juice
Butter

1 Lay fish fillets on a plate.	
2 Sprinkle with salt and pepper.	
3 Add a dab of butter and a squeeze of lemon juice.	
4 Cover with plastic film.	*Cook 2 minutes for each fillet.*
5 If cooking larger quantities use suitable dish.	*Cook, turning every 2 minutes.*

This recipe is good for the invalid or the elderly. Any white fish fillet is suitable but thicker cuts will take longer to cook. The fish is cooked when it appears white with a milky liquid escaping.

Smoked Haddock

Wash haddock and place in a shallow suitable
   casserole.
Dot with butter if liked and cover with plastic
   film.

*Cook 6 minutes,
turning dish every 2
minutes. Test after 4
minutes to be sure not
to overcook.*

Smoked cod or haddock fillet will produce the same results.
    Left-overs can be mixed with cooked rice and peas and bound
with a little mayonnaise to provide a well-balanced salad supper.
    Cooking times may vary according to the size of the fish.

Kippers

1 pair kippers
$\frac{1}{4}$ tsp cayene papper

1   Remove heads and tails with kitchen scissors.
2   Lay in base of suitable sized dish or on a
     dinner plate.
3   Sprinkle with pepper.
4   Cover with plastic film.

*Cook 4 minutes
approximately, turning
dish after 2 minutes*

Cooking time will depend on the size of the kippers. Kipper fillets
will take a similar time, but canned kipper fillets and boil-in-the-
bag kipper fillets will cook slightly quicker. Boil-in-the-bag kipper
fillets may be emptied into a suitable dish for cooking in the oven.

Sautéed Prawns in Brandy and Cream

6 oz (170 g) cooked, shelled prawns   Salt, pepper
$\frac{3}{4}$ oz (20 g) butter $\frac{1}{4}$ level tsp grated nutmeg
Scant $\frac{1}{4}$ pt (150 ml) cream   1 tsp chopped fresh parsley
2 tsp brandy   2 oz (60 g) cooked long-grained rice

1   Place butter in suitable casserole with prawns.   *Cook 1 minute. Stir.
Cook 2 minutes.*

2 Add salt, pepper, nutmeg and parsley.	*Cook 1 minute.*
3 Add brandy. Stir well.	*Cook 1 minute.*
4 Stir in cream.	*Cook to boiling point 1 minute approx.*
5 Place rice on non-metallic serving dish.	*Cook 2 minutes to re-heat rice.*
6 Top with prawn mixture.	

Serve immediately.

This dish is expensive, but a good starter for that special dinner party. Buy prawns in large packs from frozen-food shops and keep them in your freezer, using them as required. Prawns purchased in small packets can cost up to twice as much.

Tomato Prawn Savoury

1 oz (30 g) butter or margarine
1 onion
1 green pepper
1 oz (30 g) flour
1 14-oz (400-g) can of tomatoes, strained, or 4 large tomatoes and 1 tbsp tomato purée
1 tsp oregano
$\frac{1}{4}$ pt (150 ml) dry white wine
2 tbsp frozen peas
1 tsp sugar
$\frac{1}{2}$ lb (230 g) fresh or frozen peeled prawns
Salt, pepper

1 Melt butter in suitable casserole.	*Cook 30 seconds.*
2 Peel and chop the onion, remove core and pips from pepper and chop finely.	
3 Add onion and peppers to butter.	*Cook 3 minutes, stirring after 1½ minutes.*
4 Stir in flour.	
5 Add tomatoes, peas, oregano, salt, pepper and sugar.	*Cook 3 minutes.*
6 Add wine and prawns.	*Cook 2 to 3 minutes.*

Seafood cooks extremely well in the oven. Substitute shrimps or scampi or use a mixture in this recipe.
Serve hot on a bed of rice.
Enough for 4.

9 Meat and Poultry

This chapter includes roasting times for beef, pork, lamb, veal, turkey and chicken. The instructions for defrosting, if followed carefully, will enable you to serve cooked joints within an hour of removal from the freezer. Most of the dishes are suitable for freezing. It is inadvisable to freeze chicken dishes which have been prepared from previously frozen poultry.

Always use the best quality available. The microwave will not tenderize tough cuts, although some cheaper meat may be made more palatable by pre-treating, such as soaking in a marinade. Minced beef or lamb will cook well, the fibres having been broken down in the mincing process.

Large joints will brown but smaller pieces, such as steaks and chops, should be browned under a grill. Meat is more likely to brown if cooked uncovered, but you must expect to lose moisture in the process.

The utter simplicity and cleanliness of cooking meat and poultry in the microwave compensates for any lack in texture. Overcooking will not soften flesh, so do not be tempted to lengthen cooking times.

Roast Beef

1 Have ready large suitable casserole to fit the meat.
2 Place undecorated saucer upside down in base of casserole.
3 Wipe joint and place on saucer.

4   Cover with lid.

Cook 6 to 8 minutes per pound. Turn joint over midway through cooking.

5   Leave 10 minutes before serving.
6   Turn on to carving dish, slice and serve.

Roast Lamb

Cook as above 9 minutes per pound.

Roast Pork

Cook as above 10 minutes per pound.

Roast Veal

Cook as above 8½ minutes per pound.

To Thaw Frozen Meat

Cook 2 minutes and rest 15 minutes, repeating as necessary.

Whole Roast Chicken

1   Wash and clean the inside of the chicken. Rub all over with olive oil.
2   Place in large suitable casserole with lid.

Cook, allowing 5 to 6 minutes per pound (450 g), turning casserole occasionally.

3   Allow to stand 5 minutes before carving. An average chicken takes 15 to 20 minutes. Serve with pre-roasted potatoes re-heated in the oven.

To Thaw a Frozen Chicken

1   Remove wrappings and place on a glass dish.
2   Place in oven.

Cook to thaw 1 minute per pound (450 g).

3   Turn chicken upside down.

Cook to thaw a further 1 minute per pound (450 g).

4   Remove from oven. Remove bag of giblets. Wash ready for cooking.

Chicken should not be cooked from a frozen state as this toughens the flesh and impairs the flavour.

Roast Turkey

Allow $\frac{1}{2}$ lb (230 g) prepared turkey for each person.
1 Make sure that the turkey is not too large to
   go into the oven.
2 Prepare stuffing. Stuff the cleaned turkey from
   both ends.
3 Rub olive oil all over the turkey.
4 Place on a large suitable dish.
5 Cook 6 to 7 minutes per pound (450 g)
   turning and basting occasionally.
6 Allow to stand 15 minutes before carving.

Stuffing

6 oz (170 g) crustless bread
3 oz (90 g) margarine
3 standard eggs (beaten)
Salt, pepper
3 tbsp chopped fresh parsley
$1\frac{1}{2}$ tsp mixed dried herbs
Grated rind of 1 lemon

1 Soak bread in egg and mash.
2 Mix in softened margarine.
3 Add remainder of ingredients and remember to
   season well.

This amount will serve 12.

Chestnut stuffing

1 lb (450 g) chestnuts
$\frac{1}{2}$ pt ($\frac{1}{4}$ lit) water and 1 chicken stock cube or $\frac{1}{2}$ pt ($\frac{1}{4}$ lit) stock
1 oz (30 g) margarine
$\frac{1}{2}$ tsp sugar
Pinch of mixed spice
Salt, pepper

1 Boil chestnuts. Shell and skin.
2 Cook chestnuts in stock until soft.
3 Drain and mash.
4 Melt butter. Add to chestnuts with seasoning,
   spices and sugar.
5 Moisten with sufficient stock to make slightly
   sticky.

This can be cooked either on a conventional hob or in the oven,
but there is no appreciable saving of time in using the latter.

To Thaw Frozen Turkey

1 Place turkey on suitable dish and place in oven.	*Cook ½ minute per pound (450 g)*
2 Turn turkey upside down.	*Cook ½ minute per pound (450 g).*
3 Leave to rest 15 minutes before cleaning.	

Beef Braisé

1 lb (450 g) good-quality braising steak	1 Oxo cube (red)
1 medium onion	1 beef stock cube
1 tbsp seasoned flour	½ pt (¼ lit) water

1 Wipe and trim the steak, cut into 4 pieces.
2 Tenderize by making criss-cross cuts over both
  surfaces with a sharp knife.

Tenderizing steak

3 Chop onion finely and place in suitable casserole with oil.	*Cook 2 minutes.*
4 Coat meat with seasoned flour.	
5 Add meat to casserole and baste with onion mixture.	*Cook 5 minutes.*
6 Add crumbled Oxo and stock cubes and add water.	*Cook 5 minutes.*
7 Stir well to distribute flavourings evenly.	
8 Cover.	*Cook 10 to 15 minutes, stirring occasionally.*

Timing will depend on the thickness and quality of the meat.

When using stock cubes be careful not to add too much salt.

To coat quickly with seasoned flour, place flour, salt and pepper in a polythene bag and drop pieces of meat in one at a time. Hold the bag closed and shake.

This method saves the mess of sticky flour everywhere.

Hamburgers

1 lb (450 g) lean minced beef
Salt, pepper
1 heaped tsp chopped parsley
1 large potato
1 large onion

$\frac{1}{2}$ tsp mixed herbs (optional)
1 tsp Worcestershire sauce
1 tsp tomato purée
Pinch of mustard (dry)

1 Put meat in basin.
2 Add grated onion, chopped parsley, salt, pepper, herbs, Worcestershire sauce, tomato purée and mustard.
3 Lastly grate in raw peeled potato.
4 Mix thoroughly and form into flat cakes (8).
5 Place in oven on kitchen paper, 4 at a time, evenly spaced round centre.

Cook 3 minutes each hamburger. 10 minutes for 4 hamburgers.

Hamburgers are usually served with soft rolls. Cut the rolls in half and place the hamburger in between. If you want to serve them together hot, place for 45 seconds in the microwave.

Try hamburgers in a split jacket potato and sprinkle with grated cheese.

Hamburgers are cooked on the paper to absorb surplus fat.

Langdon Blanket

1 2-in-thick slice of good-quality braising steak or cheap-quality frying steak, weight – 2 lb (1 kg)
2 oz (60 g) mushrooms
1 small onion
1 small aubergine
1 tsp Worcestershire sauce
1 tbsp tomato ketchup

Salt, pepper
Squeeze of garlic powder
Olive oil

1 roaster bag and short length of string
String for securing meat

1 Wipe and trim steak. Cut horizontally so that
  you have two long steaks about 1 in thick each.
2 Batten both steaks with a meat hammer or a
  rolling pin.
3 Peel and chop mushrooms, aubergines and
  onions.
4 Mix vegetables with sauce, ketchup, garlic and
  seasoning.
5 Place vegetable mixture evenly over 1 steak.
6 Cover with other slice of steak and tie securely
  at 2-in intervals around. Tie another piece of
  string around lengthways.

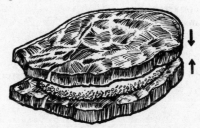

Tying stuffed beef.

1   Place one piece of steak over another that has been covered with
stuffing, thus making a sandwich.   2   Tie strings round the sandwich at
2-in intervals and one string along its length.

7 Rub meat all over with olive oil and place in a
  roaster bag.
8 Tie open end of roaster bag with string.
  DO NOT USE THE METAL TIES PROVIDED.
9 Place in glass roasting dish.

Cook 12 minutes approx.

10 Allow to stand 5 minutes, then open roaster
   bag and turn into dish.

47

11 Remove string and serve carved in 1-in-thick
  slices with the natural gravy surrounding the
  joint.

A change from the traditional Sunday joint, this method of
cooking retains the juices from the meat.

Roaster bags can be obtained from large stores or newsagents
and are generally packed in boxes of 8.

Shepherd's Pie

½ lb (230 g) minced cooked beef
1 lb (450 g) cooked mashed potato
2 tsp flour
1 small onion
2 tomatoes
½ pt (¼ lit) water and ½ beef stock cube OR ½ pt (¼ lit) stock
1 Oxo cube
Salt, pepper

1 Chop onion finely and place in suitable dish
  with water and cube or stock.   *Cook 4 minutes.*
2 Crumble in Oxo cube and seasoning (not too
  much salt).
3 Lightly mix flour with minced beef and stir
  into onion mixture.
4 Place tomatoes whole but pricked into meat
  mixture.   *Cook 10 minutes.*
                                                    Turn dish ¼ turn
                                                    every 2½ minutes.

5. Prepare freshly mashed or re-constituted potato
   and smooth on top of meat. Mark with a fork.
6 Place under pre-heated grill to brown.

Care should be taken to eat when cooked as bacteria multiply
quickly in cooked meat and so it is inadvisable to pre-cook and
then re-heat shepherd's pie a second time.

If shepherd's pie is to be frozen omit cooking time at stage 4
and leave browning until ready to eat.

Freeze in polypropylene dishes and not in foil containers.
The dishes can then go straight into the oven for 10 minutes
approx. to cook.

Steak with Green Peppers (Chinese Style)

1 lb (450 g) good quality lean steak	$\frac{1}{4}$ level tsp ground ginger
3 tbsp olive oil	1 level tsp cornflour
$\frac{1}{4}$ Spanish onion	$\frac{1}{4}$ pt (150 ml) water
Squeeze of garlic powder	$\frac{1}{2}$ beef stock cube
1 green pepper	3 tsp soy sauce
Salt, pepper	

1 Remove any fat from meat and discard.
2 Tenderize the meat by hitting with a meat beater
   or a rolling pin.
3 Cut into thin strips 2 x $\frac{1}{4}$ x $\frac{1}{4}$ in.
4 Chop onion and green pepper finely.
5 Place oil in suitable dish with onion and pepper.
   Cover. *Cook for 5 minutes.*
6 Add meat strips and salt and pepper. *Cook for 15 minutes, stirring every 5 minutes.*

7 Blend cornflour with cold water. Add garlic
   powder, ground ginger, soy sauce and crumbled
   stock cube. Add to meat dish. *Cook for 4 minutes; stir after 2 minutes.*

The Chinese quick-stir fry method of cooking can be used whenever time is short. The vegetables remain crisp with a maximum
retention of vitamins.

Curry (basic recipe)

$3\frac{1}{2}$ lb (2 kg) chicken, jointed	1 tsp lemon juice
2 onions	1 tsp tomato paste
1 tbsp curry powder	Small carton (5 oz/145 g) natural yoghourt
2 oz (60 g) cooking fat	$\frac{1}{4}$ pt (150 ml) water or stock
Salt, pepper, garlic	

1 Prepare the chicken, wash and clean, remove
   surplus skin.
2 Chop onions finely and place with fat in
   suitable casserole. *Cook 5 minutes, stirring every 2 minutes.*

3 Add curry powder, salt, pepper and garlic. *Cook 2 minutes.*
4 Add chicken. *Cook 3 minutes.*
5 Add water, lemon juice and tomato paste. *Cook 10 minutes. Turn chicken pieces over after 5 minutes.*

6 Blend in yoghourt — if lumps are not dis-
   solved they will not mix during cooking.   *Cook 10 minutes,*
                                                      basting chicken twice.

7 Add more water to sauce if it is too thick. If
   the sauce is too insipid it is probable that not
   enough salt was added.

Chicken joints vary in size and shape and therefore it is not possible to give exact timings.

Use this recipe for beef or lamb but the quality must be good and the pieces must be cut up very small. Cooking time before adding the yoghourt should be lengthened to 20 minutes.

Serve with poppadums, chapatis, dahl and curried mixed vegetables.

Chapatis

½ lb (230 g) wholemeal flour   ½ tsp salt
¼ pt (150 ml) cold water

1 Mix flour, water and salt to form a stiff dough.
2 Knead well.
3 Cover and rest for ½ hour.
4 Form into balls and roll into pancake shapes.
5 Cook one at a time on vegetable parchment.   *1½ minutes approx.*

Chapatis are Indian bread containing no raising agent. They are eaten as an accompaniment to curry dishes. Chapatis can be deep-frozen and then re-heated in the oven for ½ minute.

Poppadums

Poppadums   Greaseproof paper
Salad oil

1 Brush each poppadum on both sides with oil.
2 Place on greaseproof paper in oven.   *Cook 1 minute.*
3 Drain on absorbent paper.

Poppadums are served with curries, sometimes as a starter with lime pickle. They are crisp crackers to nibble while waiting for the main course. They are obtainable at some supermarkets and all

Indian and Pakistani grocers in packs of 20 to 30; they can be plain or spiced. When cooked they grow and puff up at the edges and, after draining, they can be kept in a large well-secured polythene bag in the refrigerator for a few days.

Chicken Paprika

1 3½-lb (2 kg) chicken
1 tsp curry powder
1 level tsp salt
1 level tsp ground ginger
2 crushed cloves of garlic or squeeze of garlic
   powder
2 tsp paprika (good-quality sweet paprika if
   possible)
1 carton natural yoghourt

1 Wash the chicken thoroughly.
2 Rub chicken all over with paprika.
3 Mix ground ginger, curry powder, garlic and
   salt with yoghourt.
4 Place chicken in a suitable casserole and pour
   the yoghourt mixture over. Leave for 2 hours,
   basting with mixture occasionally.
5 Cover.   *Cook for 20 minutes,*
                                       turning dish every
                                       5 minutes.
6 Baste before serving.

Chicken should be left 5 to 10 minutes before serving to allow the heat to distribute itself evenly through the bird.

This dish is equally attractive cooked with chicken pieces.

Allow frozen chicken to defrost first.

Individual chicken portions require about 6 to 7 minutes cooking time.

Chicken in Turmeric Sauce

4 chicken joints   2 oz (60 g) soft margarine
1 chicken stock cube   2 oz (60 g) plain flour

1 pt ($\frac{1}{2}$ lit) water or water and chicken liquor mixed
1 heaped tbsp instant dried milk
Salt, pepper
Garlic powder
$\frac{1}{2}$ tsp ground ginger
1 level tsp turmeric

1 Skin and wash chicken joints and sprinkle with
   salt and pepper, a tiny tiny squeeze of garlic
   powder and $\frac{1}{2}$ tsp ground ginger.
2 Place in a large suitable casserole with lid.

Cook 20 minutes.
Test after 15 minutes
as joints may vary in size.

3 Remove from oven and leave to cool.
4 Prepare sauce — put flour and dried milk in
   suitable casserole and gradually add $\frac{3}{4}$ pt
   (225 ml) cold water, blending carefully so that
   there are no lumps.
5 Add margarine but do not break up.
6 Add stock cube whole.
7 Cook in oven until thick.

Cook 4 minutes,
stirring every 1 minute.

8 Mix in turmeric and salt and pepper to taste.

9 Thin mixture down to cooking consistency with
   about $\frac{1}{4}$ pt (150 ml) of liquor from cooked
   chicken.
10 Cover with damp greaseproof paper wet side
   down, to prevent a skin from forming.
11 Cut flesh away from chicken bones, using a
   sharp knife and a chopping board. Cut into
   large chunks and add to sauce.
12 Re-heat in oven for 2 to 3 minutes
   before serving

This dish, which is a rich creamy yellow colour, is attractive
served on a bed of rice and accompanied by a green vegetable
such as peas or whole French beans. The rice, which can be pre-
cooked, may be re-heated with the chicken.

Roast Chicken with Almonds

$3\frac{1}{2}$ lb (2 kg) chicken
2 oz (60 g) butter
1 level tsp dried tarragon

$\frac{1}{2}$ pt ($\frac{1}{4}$ lit) water
$\frac{1}{2}$ chicken stock cube
2 oz (60 g) blanched almonds

1½ oz (45 g) flour
Salt, pepper
Pinch of sugar

Pinch of ground mace
2 tbsp cream

1 Prepare and joint chicken.

Jointing a chicken

1 Halve chicken along breast-bone. 2 Press here to separate leg and
wing.
Cut along line of arrow.

2 Place ½ oz (15 g) butter in a suitable casserole. *Melt 20 seconds.*
3 Add almonds, stir and cover. *Cook 2½ minutes.*
4 Remove almonds from casserole and set aside.
5 Rub 1½ oz (45 g) butter and tarragon over
chicken joints.
6 Place in casserole, cover with lid. *Cook 20 minutes*
approx., turning
chicken joints over
occasionally.

7 Remove chicken joints from casserole and keep
warm.
8 Blend in flour with ½ pt (¼ lit) cold water and
place in same casserole with chicken juices, *Cook 5 minutes,*
stock cube, mace, sugar and seasoning. *stirring occasionally.*

9 Add almonds and cream to sauce.
10 Place chicken on serving dish and pour sauce
over.

Crumbed Loin of Lamb

1 2½-lb (1-kg) joint, loin or best end neck of lamb
2 standard eggs
4 oz (110 g) breadcrumbs
Salt, pepper

1 Wash lamb and trim away any surplus fat.
2 Beat eggs with seasoning.

3 Coat joint all over with beaten egg and dip in
   breadcrumbs.
4 Repeat with remaining egg and breadcrumbs.
5 Place joint in suitable dish and cook uncovered.   *Cook 20 minutes.*
                                                      Turn joint over after
                                                      10 minutes.

6 If desired brown under a pre-heated grill.

To coat large pieces of fish or meat with breadcrumbs spread
the crumbs on a sheet of greaseproof paper, lay meat or fish in
centre and press remainder of crumbs on top with a palette knife.

Casserole of Lamb's Liver

6 slices lamb's liver   Salt, pepper
10 spring onions or 1 medium onion   1 tsp tomato purée
1 tsp Bovril   1 tbsp water

1 Wash liver in cold, salted water, removing skin
   and membranes.
2 Season with salt and pepper and place in
   suitable casserole.
3 Put coarsely chopped onion or spring onions
   whole on top of the liver.
4 Blend Bovril, tomato purée and water and
   pour over.
5 Place lid on casserole.   *Cook 7 minutes,*
                                            turning after 3
                                            minutes and testing
                                            after 5 minutes.

The casserole should be turned a half turn to ensure even cooking.
Re-heat before serving for about *3 minutes.*
Creamed potatoes (fresh or instant) complement this simple
dish, which is ideal when a member of the family calls in
unexpectedly at lunch-time.
Liver is rich in iron.

Liver and Bacon Terrine

12 oz (350 g) joint of lean cooked bacon   3 oz (90 g) margarine
4 oz (110 g) liver   4 oz (110 g) breadcrumbs

1 onion	1 standard egg
4 or 5 shakes of pepper	$\frac{1}{4}$ pt (150 ml) milk
1 level tsp mixed herbs	

1 Mince bacon, liver and onion.
2 Stir in 2 oz (60 g) of the breadcrumbs, mixed herbs and pepper.
3 Beat egg into milk and add to mixture.
4 Melt margarine in frying pan and gently fry remaining 2 oz (60 g) of breadcrumbs until golden on a conventional hob.
5 Press 1½ oz (45 g) of the golden breadcrumbs around the base of a suitable loaf dish or casserole.
6 Turn bacon mixture into dish and press down well.
7 Cover with remaining golden breadcrumbs and place a sheet of greaseproof paper on top.

Cook 12 minutes approx., turning casserole a $\frac{1}{4}$ turn every 2½ minutes.

This looks attractive served in the casserole but may be turned on to a heated serving platter if desired.

Remember to divide the breadcrumbs carefully, leaving enough for each stage.

Serves 4 to 6.

Liver Pâté

6 oz (170 g) lamb's liver	1 bayleaf
2 oz (60 g) back bacon	3 to 4 peppercorns (white)
$\frac{1}{2}$ crushed clove of garlic	$\frac{1}{2}$ pt ($\frac{1}{4}$ lit) milk
1 tsp anchovy essence	1 oz (30 g) butter
1 slice onion	1 oz (30 g) flour
2 blades mace	Salt, pepper

1 Heat milk in suitable jug with onion, mace, bayleaf and peppercorns. *Cook 1½ minutes.*
2 Remove from oven, cover and set aside to infuse. *15 to 30 minutes.*
3 Mince liver and bacon twice.
4 Add crushed garlic and anchovy essence.
5 Strain milk into a jug. Throw away vegatables and herbs.
6 Melt butter in clean, suitable casserole in oven. *$\frac{1}{2}$ minute.*

7 Blend in flour.

                                              Cook ½ minute.

8 Add milk carefully and stir well, season to
   taste.

                                              Cook 2 minutes.

9 Add sauce to minced mixture.

10 Press mixture into six small dishes.

11 Place six dishes in large dish half-filled with
   boiling water.

                                              Cook 15 minutes,
altering the position of
the dishes every 3
minutes.

12 Leave to cool. Refrigerate until required.

Serve in the dishes with hot toast and butter.

Savoury Liver

¾ lb (340 g) liver
1 or 2 onions
1 tbsp seasoned flour
4 oz (110 g) fresh breadcrumbs
4 to 6 rashers streaky bacon
1 tbsp chopped fresh parsley
½ tsp dried mixed herbs
Salt, pepper, nutmeg
¼ pt (150 ml) stock or water
2 pt (1 lit) casserole

1 Wash liver in cold, salted water.
2 Trim slices and remove blood vessels.
3 Toss in seasoned flour.
4 Lay liver in casserole.
5 Pour stock over liver to cover.
6 Grate onion on coarse grater.
7 Mix onion with breadcrumbs, herbs, pinch of
   nutmeg, salt and pepper.
8 Place breadcrumb mixture on liver.
9 Remove rinds from bacon.
10 Lay bacon rashers over breadcrumb mixture
   in casserole.
11 Keep casserole covered with greaseproof paper
   to prevent spattering.

                                              Cook 15 minutes,
turning casserole every
5 minutes.

Sprinkle with parsley before serving.
Suitable accompaniments are Vichy carrots and broccoli spears.
Serves 4.

Rognon Sauté Vin Rouge

½ lb (230 g) kidney (ox or lamb) 1 tbsp olive oil
1 level tbsp flour 3 tbsp red wine
Salt, pepper 3 tbsp water

1 Wash the kidneys in cold salt water and remove
   any membrane or core.
2 Cut into pieces (each lamb's kidney into four).
3 Place flour, salt and pepper in a polythene bag
   and toss the kidneys in this.
4 Place the oil in base of a suitable casserole and
   turn kidney mixture into this. *Cook uncovered for
   5 minutes, stirring
   frequently.*

5 Add wine and water to kidneys and mix well.
   Cover. *Cook for 10 minutes,
   stirring occasionally.*

Since kidney is offal it must be very thoroughly cleansed before
cooking; carcass meat needs only to be wiped with a damp cloth.

Any red wine is suitable and it is possible to obtain variations
by using a sweet wine such as Marsala for a round smooth flavour
or a dry Bordeaux for a more piquant taste.

Barbecued Spare Ribs

1 lb (450 g) pork spare ribs 1 oz (30 g) butter
1 tbsp olive oil Squeeze of garlic powder
¼ pt (150 ml) tomato ketchup 2 tbsp vinegar
1 tbsp water Juice of ½ lemon
1 tbsp brown sugar ½ tsp paprika
1 tbsp Worcestershire sauce 1 tsp soy sauce

1 In a suitable bowl mix all ingredients except
   spare ribs to form a sauce. Stir well. *Cook 3½ minutes.*
2 Stir well.
3 Place spare ribs in suitable casserole. Cover. *Cook 4 minutes.*
4 Turn over. *Cook 2 minutes.*
5 Pour sauce over meat. *Cook 4 minutes approx.*
6 Test meat with fork, which should easily
   penetrate flesh.
7 Leave to stand for 5 minutes before serving.

Spare ribs have become popular since there has been the oppor-
tunity to try them in Chinese restaurants.

Barbecue sauce, which is pungent, may accompany any meat or poultry.

Serve this dish with hot rice.

Enough for 2.

Sweet and Sour Pork

1 thinly sliced carrot
1 thinly sliced onion
1 tbsp cooking oil
8 oz (230 g) can pineapple pieces.
¼ pt (150 ml) juice and water mixed
Grated rind and juice of 1 lemon
¼ pt (150 ml) malt vinegar
2 tsp soy sauce

3 oz (90 g) dark brown sugar
2 level tsp cornflour
2 tbsp water
Salt, pepper
1 lb (450 g) lean pork
1 large egg
2 tsp flour mixed with 2 tsp cornflour
Deep fat for frying

1 Place carrot and onion in oil in casserole.   *Cook 4 minutes, stirring after 2 minutes.*

2 Add pineapple, juice and water, vinegar, lemon juice, grated rind, soy sauce and sugar.   *Cook 4 minutes.*

3 Blend cornflour with 2 tbsp water. Blend with sauce in casserole.   *Cook to thicken 2 minutes.*

4 Season.
5 Cut meat into cubes.
6 Make a batter with egg, flour and cornflour.
7 Dip meat cubes into batter and fry in deep fat on a conventional hob at a temperature of 360°F (180°C) for about 10 minutes, until pork is thoroughly cooked.
8 Drain meat. Place in serving dish and pour hot sauce over.

If no thermometer is available the temperature of the oil may be tested by frying a small cube of dry bread. This should take 30 seconds to turn golden.

Braised Honey Ham

8 oz (230 g) slice cooked gammon or ham steak
2 tbsp thin honey

1 tbsp lemon juice
Watercress for garnish

1 Place ham in suitable dish.
2 Mix honey with lemon juice and pour over ham,
  cover with greaseproof paper.   *Cook 3 minutes.*
                                              Turn gammon over after
                                              1½ minutes and baste.

3 Serve hot accompanied by freshly cooked peas
  or french beans.

Quick Sausage Supper

1 lb (450 g) large sausages	Small can of chick peas
1 packet dried onion soup	½ pt (¼ lit) water

1 Blend soup powder with water and place in a
  suitable casserole.   *Cook 4 minutes,*
                                              stirring every minute.

2 Slit sausages down one side and place in soup,
  slit side down.
3 Cover.   *Cook 10 minutes,*
                                              turning sausages
                                              frequently.
4 Drain chick peas and stir into sauce.   *Cook 2 minutes.*
5 Serve hot.

Chick peas are not generally eaten in this country, but are available at continental grocers. They are the size of hazel-nuts and a light beige colour, with a distinctive flavour.

Sausages

3 large beef or pork sausages	Kitchen paper

1 Prick the sausages well.
2 Place on kitchen paper on a suitable dish and
  cover with another sheet of kitchen paper. *Cook 1½ minutes*
                                              approx. per sausage.
                                              Turn over half way
                                              through cooking time.

Sausages continue to cook after the oven is switched off. It is advisable to allow them to stand a few minutes before eating.
Sausages in 1-lb (450-g) packs straight from the food-freezer

should be placed in the oven for 2 minutes. They will then be ready to separate, whereupon cooking may be completed.

Baked Beans on Toast

1 slice of buttered toast 1 small can of baked beans

1 Open can of beans and empty contents into a small suitable dish.
2 Heat in oven until hot. *Cook 1½ minutes approx.*
3 Place on a slice of buttered toast on a non-trimmed dinner plate *Cook 15 seconds*

If desired top with very thin slices of tomato when re-heating.

Sausage and Tomato Casserole

1¼ lb (680 g) pork or beef sausage meat. 1 (1 lb 13 oz/830 g) can of tomatoes.
1 oz (30 g) flour Pinch of dried basil.
2 large onions. Salt, pepper.

1 Using floured hands, roll sausage meat into 12 balls.
2 Toss balls in remainder of flour.
3 Place in suitable casserole and cover with canned tomatoes and liquor. Season.
4 Peel and thinly slice onions. Turn on to sausage mixture.
5 Sprinkle basil on top. *Cook for 20 minutes approx. Turn dish ¼ turn every 4 minutes.*

This recipe will serve 4–6.
An easy dish for a "last-minute" meal.

Blanquette de Veau

1 lb (450 g) veal 1 oz (30 g) butter
1 large onion 1 oz (30 g) flour
Bouquet garni 1 tbsp cream

1 egg yolk   Pepper, salt.
6 button bushrooms (canned)

1 Cut veal into small pieces.
2 Peel and slice onion.
3 Place veal and onion in suitable casserole.
4 Cover with cold salted water.   *Cook 10 minutes.*
5 Skim if necessary.
6 Add bouquet garni.   *Cook 20 minutes,*
                                                 stirring occasionally.

7 Test and continue cooking if necessary.
8 Strain off stock and reserve. Remove bouquet
   garni.
9 Place veal on serving dish and keep hot.
10 Place butter in casserole.   *Cook 1 minute.*
11 Blend in flour.   *Cook ½ minute.*
12 Add stock gradually. Make up to ¾ pt (225 ml)
   with water. Beat well, season.   *Cook 4 minutes,*
                                                 stirring every 1
                                                 minute.

13 Mix cream with egg-yolk and add to sauce.
14 Return to oven for a few seconds but do not
   boil.
15 Strain sauce over veal.
16 Garnish with sliced mushrooms.

Serve hot with fleurons of puff pastry.

Bouquet garni is a bunch of herbs tied in muslin. While it is
convenient to buy them in ready-prepared sachets, it is much
cheaper to make them yourself.

Cut 2-in squares of muslin and place a blade of mace, 2 or 3
white peppercorns, a pinch of dried parsley, a pinch of thyme and
a crushed bayleaf in the centre. Gather all the edges of the muslin
together and tie securely with a strip of muslin or cotton. Trim
away surplus muslin. Keep in a jar with a screw top.

Veal Beaujolais

8 thin slices escalope veal   ⅛ pt (70 ml) water
1 tbsp olive oil   4 oz (110 g) mushrooms, thickly sliced
1 small, finely chopped onion   ½ chicken stock cube
½ oz (15 g) flour   Salt, pepper
¼ pt (150 ml) Beaujolais

1 Mix onion with oil in casserole.   *Cook 3 minutes.*

2 Blend in flour.   *Cook 1 minute.*
3 Add wine and water, stir well, cook until sauce
   thickens.   *2 minutes.*
4 Add mushrooms, stock cube and seasoning.   *Cook 2 minutes.*
5 Lay sliced veal in sauce and baste, cover.   *Cook 15 minutes,*
                                                      stirring every 5 minutes.

The sauce should be the consistency of cream and it may be necessary to thin it down with a little more water.

Veal Beaujolais is suitable for deep freezing. Re-heating will depend on the size of the portion.

10 Pastas and Rice

Pasta is a mixture of flour and water, kneaded into a paste, rolled, dried and cut into the required lengths or shapes. Pasta may be made at home but the drying-out process is lengthy and the paste may fill the surface area of a large table.

Macaroni and spaghetti are stocked by most grocers, but should you require a more unusual variety it is better to try a continental grocer or one in a cosmopolitan area. Among those available in this country are tagliatelli noodles, which can be in the form of nests or thin folded strips, and made with or without egg. Canneloni, which is usually stuffed and served with a coating sauce, is available in different-sized tubes or flat squares for making your own tubes. Chinese noodles are very narrow round lengths of pasta which are intertwined and may be boiled or used for crispy noodles. Lasagne, white or green, is the foundation of a now popular dish incorporating a meat and cheese sauce. Small pasta pieces for use in soups come in alphabet shapes, squares and stars, and an even smaller variety is useful for soups for babies and invalids.

Manufacturers are currently producing quick-cook pastas in different forms and this considerably cuts down the cooking time.

Uncooked pasta keeps well and has a long shelf-life. It is an inexpensive base for many dishes.

When cooking by microwave be sure that the pasta is submerged in the water. Any pieces protruding will become brown and brittle. A little butter in the cooking water will help to keep the pieces separate. In the microwave oven it is possible to boil some pastas from a cold water start, but if in doubt, it is better and quicker to start with boiling water.

When purchasing rice, consider which dishes you will be preparing and choose the most suitable variety. Round-grain rice is suitable for sweet dishes and long-grain for savoury dishes. Round-grain rice is more gelatinous and amalgamates with milk or water to form a pudding. Long-grain rice, if properly cooked, will remain separate. Patna and Basmatti rice should be thoroughly washed in cold water before use, but American long-grain rice is pre-cleaned and may be used direct from the packet. "Easy cook" rice, which has been specially processed, appears to have larger grains and requires more water when cooking. Also available is instant rice which has been dehydrated and is easy to re-constitute, and health-food shops stock brown rice, which is said to have more vitamin retention.

Macaroni Cheese

3 oz (90 g) quick macaroni	$\frac{3}{4}$ oz (20 g) flour
Dab of butter	Pinch of mustard
$\frac{1}{2}$ tsp salt	Salt, pepper
$\frac{1}{2}$ pt ($\frac{1}{4}$ lit) milk	3 oz (90 g) grated hard cheese
$\frac{3}{4}$ oz (20 g) butter or margarine	

1 Place macaroni in suitable casserole. Cover with water and add salt, add a dab of butter.   *Cook until nearly tender, 5 minutes approx. Stir occasionally.*

2 Drain and run through with cold water.
3 Melt $\frac{3}{4}$ oz (20 g) butter in a casserole.   *20 seconds.*
4 Add flour and stir.   *Cook 30 seconds.*
5 Gradually blend in milk.
6 Add salt and pepper to taste. Add mustard.   *Cook 4 minutes, stirring every 1 minute.*

7 Stir in two-thirds of cheese.
8 Toss in drained macaroni.   *Re-heat 1 minute.*
9 Sprinkle with remaining grated cheese.
10 Brown under grill if desired.

If this dish is to be re-heated the sauce should be thinned down with milk as sauces tend to thicken when left standing.

A green salad is a good accompaniment for macaroni cheese.

For a change use spaghetti, or tagliatelli.

Coloured cheddar or red Leicester cheese, used instead of a white cheese, will give a warmer appearance.

Lasagne

4 oz (110 g) pasta – green or white
$\frac{1}{2}$ oz (15 g) margarine
Meat sauce
1 small chopped onion
Squeeze of garlic powder or crushed clove of garlic
1 oz (30 g) margarine
Bayleaf
4 oz (110 g) minced lean beef
2 medium tomatoes
$\frac{1}{2}$ beef stock cube
$\frac{1}{8}$ pt (70 ml) water
1 level tsp dried oregano
Salt, pepper
Cheese sauce
1 oz (30 g) margarine
1 oz (30 g) flour
$\frac{1}{2}$ pt ($\frac{1}{4}$ lit) milk
2 oz (60 g) grated cheese

1 Place chopped onion, garlic, bayleaf and margarine in a suitable casserole.

Cook 4 minutes

2 Add beef. Stir.

Cook 2 minutes.
Stir after 1 minute.

3 Add tomatoes, stock cube and water, oregano and seasoning.

Cook 4 minutes.
Stir after 2 minutes.

4 Remove from oven and remove bayleaf.
5 Prepare cheese sauce. Place margarine in a suitable casserole. Melt.

Cook $\frac{1}{2}$ minute.

6 Stir in flour.

Cook $\frac{1}{2}$ minute.

7 Gradually add milk.

Cook 3 minutes,
stirring every minute.

8 Stir in three-quarters of grated cheese.
9 Cook lasagne pasta. Half fill a large suitable casserole with boiling water. Add $\frac{1}{2}$ oz (15 g) margarine.

10 Bring water back to full boil.

1 to 3 minutes.

11 Place pasta leaves in water one at a time, making sure that they are fully immersed.

Cook 10 minutes
approx., testing after
6 minutes.

Pasta is ready when it will break when pressed with the side of a fork.

12 Drain and run through with water to separate the leaves.
13 Place individual leaves on a flat surface until ready to combine with the sauces.

14 Assemble. Place a layer of meat sauce in the
    bottom of a suitable dish.
15 Cover with a layer of cooked pasta.
16 Add a layer of cheese sauce.
17 Continue layers, finishing with cheese sauce.
18 Sprinkle with remaining grated cheese.
19 Place in oven.   *Cook 3 minutes.*
20 Remove from oven and brown under a pre-
    heated grill.

Lasagne will re-heat well in the oven.

In fact lasagne pasta can be cooked equally quickly and more
satisfactorily on a conventional hob, because with the oven the
leaves need to be put in individually to prevent them from sticking
together.

Luncheon Meat Cream Noodles

8 oz (230 g) quick cooking egg noodles (tagliatelli)
$\frac{1}{4}$ oz (10 g) butter or margarine
1 green pepper
1 crushed clove of garlic or squeeze of garlic powder
2 tbsp oil
6 oz (170 g) luncheon meat
2 oz (60 g) stoned black olives
3 oz (90 g) grated cheese
$\frac{1}{4}$ pt (150 ml) double cream
Salt, pepper.

1 Place noodles in large suitable casserole.
2 Cover with boiling salted water. Add butter.   *Cook 2$\frac{1}{2}$ minutes.*
3 Stir and leave for 2 or 3 minutes.
4 Slice peppers thinly and place in small covered
   casserole with garlic and oil.   *Cook 3 minutes,*
                                                      stirring after 1$\frac{1}{2}$
                                                      minutes.

5 Drain noodles and replace in casserole.
6 Add pepper mixture and olives to noodles.
7 Add cream. Season to taste.
8 Add chopped luncheon meat and cheese. Stir.   *Cook to re-heat*
                                                      2 minutes.
9 Stir and serve.

Noodles re-heat well in the oven.
Enough for a supper dish for four people.

Spaghetti alla Bolognese

8 oz (230 g) spaghetti	Bayleaf
1 tsp salt	8 oz (230 g) lean minced beef
1½ pt (1 lit) water	8 oz (230 g) can of tomatoes
¼ oz (10 g) butter or margarine	3 oz (90 g) can of tomato purée
1 onion	½ beef stock cube
Squeeze of garlic powder	Salt, pepper
1 oz (30 g) margarine	Grated cheese

Sauce

1 Place onion, garlic, bayleaf and margarine in a
   suitable casserole. — *Cook 4 minutes.*
2 Add beef. Stir. — *Cook 2 minutes.*
3 Add tomatoes, purée, stock cube and seasoning.
   Cover. — *Cook 6 minutes, stirring every 2 minutes.*

4. Remove from oven and set aside.

Spaghetti

1 Place 1½ pt (1 lit) boiling water into a suitable
   casserole.
2 Add butter. Salt to taste.
3 Lower spaghetti into water, making sure that
   the water is covering the spaghetti. — *Cook uncovered for 7 minutes approx. until just tender.*

4 Drain. Place on a suitable serving dish.
5 Pour sauce over spaghetti. Return to oven to
   re-heat. — *Cook 2 minutes.*
6 Sprinkle with grated cheese and serve hot.

If re-heating spaghetti from cold cover with a sheet of paper to avoid drying out.

Should you wish to keep cooked spaghetti without sauce, run under cold water to separate strands.

Boiled Rice

Long-grain rice	Salt
Water	

1 Wash rice well under cold water.

2 Place rice in salted water in a suitable casserole.
3 Cook uncovered. Stir occasionally.
4 When rice is cooked place in a strainer and pour
   boiling water through to separate the grains.
5 Drain well.

2 oz (60 g) rice Scant $\frac{1}{2}$ pt ($\frac{1}{4}$ lit) water Salt	*Cook 10 minutes* *approx.*
4 oz (110 g) rice $\frac{3}{4}$ pt (425 ml) water Salt	*Cook 12 minutes* *approx.*
8 oz (230 g) rice 1 pt ($\frac{1}{2}$ lit) water Salt	*Cook 14 minutes* *approx.*

Rice pilau

2 oz (60 g) onion   1 chicken stock cube
3 oz (90 g) butter   Paprika
4 oz (110 g) long-grain rice   Salt, pepper
$\frac{3}{4}$ pt (425 ml) water

1 Wash rice in a strainer and drain.	
2 Place 2 oz (60 g) butter in a suitable casserole.	*Cook 1 minute to melt.*
3 Chop onions finely and add. Stir.	*Cook 3 minutes, stirring* *every 1 minute.*
4 Add rice and mix well.	*Cook 2 minutes,* *stirring after 1 minute.*
5 Add water, stock cube, salt and pepper.	*Cook uncovered for 10* *minutes approx. Test.*
6 Leave to stand for rice to absorb all the liquid.	*10 minutes.*
7 Mix in remaining 1 oz (30 g) butter.	
8 Sprinkle with paprika.	

Serve hot with any meat dish or freeze in portions in polypropylene dishes and re-heat in oven when required. Re-heating
times will depend on the size of the portions.

Paella

4 chicken joints
1 large onion
1 crushed clove of garlic or squeeze of garlic powder

1 tbsp olive oil
8 oz (230 g) long-grain rice
1¼ pt (700 ml) stock or 1¼ pt (700 ml) water and 1 chicken stock cube
1 small can red pimientos (drained and sliced)
Pinch of saffron
8 frankfurter sausages or 8 oz (230 g) sliced salami
2 oz (60 g) prawns
2 oz (60 g) runner beans (frozen and sliced)
1 level tsp salt
Pepper

1 Place wash chicken joints in a suitable casserole. Cover.	*Cook 15 minutes. Turn chicken joints over after 7 minutes.*
2 Remove casserole from oven.	
3 Place oil in large suitable casserole. Slice the onion thinly and add. Stir.	*Cook 4 minutes.*
4 Wash and drain rice. Add to onions. Stir.	*Cook 2 minutes.*
5 Place chicken on a chopping board. Cut flesh off bone and cut into small chunks. Set aside.	
6 Measure remaining chicken juices and make up to 1¼ pt (225 ml) with hot stock or hot water and stock cube.	
7 Add hot stock, garlic, saffron, sliced pimientos, beans and seasoning to rice. Stir well.	*Cook 12 to 15 minutes until stock is absorbed, stirring occasionally.*
8 Add sliced frankfurters or salami, chicken and prawns.	*Cook 3 minutes.*

Chicken Almond Risotto

1 onion
2 oz (60 g) mushrooms
1½ (45 g) butter
4 oz (110 g) long-grain rice
1 chicken stock cube
¾ pt (425 ml) water
Salt, pepper
4 oz (110 g) cooked chicken, diced
1 oz (30 g) nib almonds

1 Melt butter.	*1 minute.*
2 Remove stalks from mushrooms, slice and add to chopped onion.	*Cook 4 minutes.*

3 Wash and drain rice and add to casserole, stir.	Cook 1½ minutes. Stir.
4 Add stock cube, boiling water and seasoning.	Cook 10 minutes approx., stirring after 5 minutes.
5 Add chopped chicken and almonds.	Re-heat for 2 minutes.

Ham, cooked chopped liver or chopped hard-boiled egg can be added instead of chicken.

11 Vegetables and Vegetable Dishes

Most fresh vegetables may be cooked in the microwave oven, but in some instances no time will be saved. What the microwave oven can do is to retain colour and crispness. Cabbage is no longer soft and stewed and has an entirely new taste and texture. Any vegetable with a high water-content will cook well and the process is hastened if the food is covered. As there is a 12 per cent water loss when using the microwave oven, a cover will help prevent the food from drying up.

Use your oven to cook all frozen vegetables or to re-heat in individual portions. Little water is required and this should be salted before adding the vegetables. Dried vegetables respond well and cooking instant potato in the microwave oven will avoid those objectionable pockets of uncooked powder.

Canned vegetables should be turned into a suitable container for re-heating and vegetables with shiny skins must be pricked well to avoid bursting. These include potatoes and tomatoes and any fruits with glossy skins.

Potatoes often blacken when cooked and set aside for a time. This blackness should disappear when they are re-heated in the microwave oven.

Vegetables for use in dishes cooked conventionally may be prepared with the aid of the oven. Mushrooms cooked for 2 minutes will be ready for use in an omelette and will not have the buttery taste that makes these omelettes so rich.

Combinations of vegetables cooked in the microwave provide interesting meals for the vegetarian; ratatouille, peperonata or courgettes and tomatoes mixed can make very interesting accompaniments for meat and fish dishes and can be served on their own, topped for example with grated cheese.

Fresh Green Beans

1 lb (450 g) green beans
¼ pt (150 ml) water
Salt

1 Prepare beans.
2 Place in a suitable casserole with salted water.
   Cover.

*Cook 14 minutes,
stirring occasionally.*

There are several varieties of green beans and each must be prepared according to its type. In general french beans should be topped, tailed and cooked whole. Runner beans should be topped and tailed and the strings down the side removed and then cut into ½-in diagonal slices.

Frozen Green Beans

8-oz (230-g) packet cut green beans
¼ pt (150 ml) hot water
Salt

OR

1 lb (450 g) packet cut green beans
¼ pt (150 ml) hot water
Salt

1 Place beans in salted water in a suitable
   casserole.
2 Cover.

*Cook 7 minutes for
8 oz (230 g). Cook 13
minutes for 1 lb (450 g),
stirring occasionally.*

Vichy Carrots

½ lb (230 g) carrots
¼ oz (15 g) butter
½ oz (15 g) sugar

Chopped parsley
⅛ pt (70 ml) water
Salt, pepper

1 Scrub, top and tail, peel or scrape the carrots.

2 Thinly slice the carrots.
3 Place in a suitable casserole with water, sugar,
   butter and seasoning.
4 Cook covered.

*Cook 8 minutes
approx., stirring twice.*

5 Sprinkle with parsley before serving.

It may be necessary to drain the carrots before serving.

Celery

1 head of celery	Salt
$\frac{1}{2}$ oz (15 g) butter	$\frac{1}{4}$ pt (150 ml) water

1 Remove green leaves and thick stalk end of
   celery.
2 Wash well in cold water. Use a brush to remove
   any earth or flies.
3 Cut into 3-in lengths and place in a suitable
   casserole with butter and $\frac{1}{4}$ pt (150 ml) hot
   salted water.
4 Cover with greaseproof paper.

*Cook 15 minutes. Turn
celery over occasionally
during cooking.*

Corn on the Cob

4 ears of corn	1 oz (30 g) butter

1 Remove outer husks and silk.
2 Place in suitable dish and dot with butter.
3 Turn corn to coat with butter. Cover.

*Cook 2 minutes.
Cook 6 minutes,
turning dish a $\frac{1}{4}$ turn
after 3 minutes and
basting occasionally.*

It is better to season after cooking as salt tends to toughen the
kernels.

Frozen Corn on the Cob

4 ears of corn	$\frac{1}{4}$ pt (150 ml) hot water

1 Place corn in suitable large casserole with water.
2 Cover.

Cook 10 minutes.
Turn dish ¼ turn every
2½ minutes.

Sweet Corn

8 oz (230 g) packet frozen sweet corn
¼ pt (150 ml) hot water

OR

1-lb (450-g) packet frozen sweet corn
¼ pt (150 ml) hot water

1 Place corn in suitable container with water.
2 Cover.

Cook 5 minutes, stirring
occasionally for ½ lb
(230 g) Cook 9
minutes, stirring
occasionally for 1 lb
(450 g)

Courgettes

1 lb (450 g) courgettes   ⅛ pt (70 ml) water
½ oz (15 g) butter   Salt

1 Wash courgettes and cut into 1-in lengths.
2 Place in suitable casserole with butter and
   salt to taste. Add water. Cover with lid.

Cook 10 minutes
approx., stirring every
5 minutes. Serves at
least 4.

Globe Artichokes

2 artichokes   *Sauce*
½ oz (15 g) butter   2 oz (60 g) salted butter
1 tbsp lemon juice   Pepper
½ tsp salt   Lemon juice if liked
½ pt (¼ lit) water

1 Wash artichokes in cold water. Remove tips of
   leaves and outside leaves.

2 Melt butter in suitable casserole in oven with salt, lemon juice and water.	*Cook to bring to boil, 4 minutes.*
3 Place artichokes in casserole.	*Cook 10 minutes approx., turning every 3 minutes.*
4 Remove and drain.	
5 Melt butter in jug with pepper and lemon juice if liked.	*Cook 1½ minutes.*
6 Pour over artichokes and serve immediately.	

Artichokes are cooked when the outer leaves tear away easily. Try artichokes cold with a vinaigrette sauce.

Frozen Peas

8 oz (230 g) frozen peas
¼ pt (150 ml) water
Salt
½ tsp castor sugar

1 Place water with salt to taste in suitable casserole.	
2 Put the frozen peas in the water.	
3 Cover with greaseproof paper.	*Cook 5 minutes.*
4 Strain and serve topped with a dot of butter.	

Cooked frozen peas re-heat well either in a casserole or on a dinner plate with other items. Re-heating will take about 1 minute.

Fresh Peas

½ lb (230 g) shelled peas   Sugar
Water   Mint
Salt

1 Put peas in suitable serving dish.	
2 Cover with boiling salted water to which has been added a pinch of sugar.	
3 Place a sprig of mint in the water.	
4 Cover with paper.	*Cook 5 minutes approx., stirring every minute.*
5 Drain and serve.	

Shredded Cabbage

1 small cabbage $\frac{1}{2}$ pt ($\frac{1}{4}$ lit) water
1 level tsp salt

1 Place salted water in suitable casserole.
2 Wash cabbage, cut into 4 and shred finely.
3 Place cabbage in prepared casserole.
4 Cover with greaseproof paper.
                                        Cook 10 minutes, stirring every 3 minutes.

5 Strain and serve.

The cabbage retains its colour and has a crispness about it that is quite different from conventionally cooked cabbage. This method of cooking lifts cabbage out of the mundane class of vegetables with which it is generally associated.

Cauliflower

1 medium cauliflower   Water
Salt

1 Wash in cold water and remove most of outside stalks.
2 Using a spoon or a grapefruit knife scoop out centre of stalk at base.
3 Using a suitable casserole that fits, half fill it with salted water.
4 Place the cauliflower in the casserole, flower side uppermost.
5 Cover.
                                        Cook 10 minutes approx. until a knife just penetrates.

Cooking time will depend on the size of the cauliflower.
Test frequently, as overcooked cauliflower will change its texture and disintegrate.

For *Cauliflower cheese* drain when nearly cooked and pour over $\frac{1}{4}$ pt ($\frac{1}{4}$ lit) cheese sauce. Top with grated cheese and brown under a grill.

Frozen Cauliflower

8-oz (230-g) packet frozen cauliflower sprigs

$\frac{1}{4}$ pt (150 ml) hot water
Salt

OR

1-lb (450-g) packet frozen cauliflower sprigs
$\frac{1}{4}$ pt (150 ml) hot water
Salt

1 Place cauliflower in a suitable casserole with
   salted water.
2 Cover.

Cook $4\frac{1}{2}$ minutes for
$\frac{1}{2}$ lb (230 g). Cook
8 minutes for 1 lb
(450 g).

Re-constituting Instant Potato

1 pt ($\frac{1}{2}$ lit) water $\frac{1}{2}$ oz (15 g) butter
5 oz (145 g) instant potato powder

1 Blend cold water with potato and stir well.
2 Add butter.

Cook 3 minutes.
Stir every 1 minute
or until water is
absorbed and the
potato thickens.

Duchesse Potatoes

Make up mixture as above but with $\frac{7}{8}$ pt ($\frac{7}{16}$ lit) water. Leave mixture to
cool and then beat in one egg-yolk. The mixture can then be piped in
swirls and browned under the grill.

Piping Duchesse potatoes

Boiled New Potatoes

$\frac{1}{2}$ lb (230 g) small potatoes, scrubbed
$\frac{1}{4}$ pt (150 ml) water
1 level tsp salt

Place potatoes in salted water, cover and cook.   *6 minutes, stirring after 3 minutes.*

• Timing must depend on the size of the cut potatoes. It is advisable to check during the cooking process to avoid overcooking.

Jacket Potatoes

1 Scrub potatoes and prick well.
2 For 2-in diameter potatoes.   *Cook 4 minutes each, turning over after 2 minutes.*

3 4 potatoes may be cooked at the same time on the oven base evenly spaced round centre.   *Cooking for 4 potatoes will be 16 minutes, turning over after 8 minutes.*

Potatoes must be thoroughly pricked to prevent bursting.
Serve split and filled with seasoned butter, grated cheese or sour cream and chopped chives.

Spinach

1 lb (450 g) washed spinach
$\frac{1}{4}$ pt (150 ml) water
Salt

1 Remove thick stem from spinach leaves. Drain well.
2 Place in large suitable casserole with salted water.
3 Cover.   *Cook 4 minutes, turning dish after 2 minutes.*

Frozen Spinach

½-lb (230-g) packet frozen leaf-spinach

1 Place spinach in suitable casserole. Cover.

*Cook 5 minutes,
breaking up spinach with
a wooden spoon after
2½ minutes.*

Spinach purée

1 small packet frozen chopped spinach   ¼ pt (150 ml) milk
½ oz (15 g) butter   Salt, pepper
½ oz (15 g) flour

1 Prepare a sauce with the milk flour and butter
   — mix the flour with the cold milk and add the
   butter.

*Cook 3 minutes,
stirring occasionally.*

2 Add block of chopped spinach ice-side up.
   Cover.

*Cook 5 minutes,
breaking up block of
spinach at frequent
intervals.*

3 Stir well.

Have this as a supper dish topped with a poached egg or cook an
egg on top for 1 minute in the oven.

Brussels Sprouts

(Fresh)

1 lb (450 g) Brussels sprouts.   Salt.
½ pt (¼ lit) water.

1 Wash sprouts in cold water and remove outer
   leaves and base.
2 Using a sharp knife, make a cross on each base.
3 Place in boiling, salted water in suitable
   casserole and cover.

*Cook 8 minutes
approx. Stir frequently.*

4 Drain and serve.

(Frozen)

1 lb (450 g) Brussels sprouts   Salt
¼ pt (150 ml) water

1 Place water and salt in suitable casserole.
2 Add sprouts. Cover.

Cook 6 to 8 minutes.
Stir after 3 minutes.

3 Drain and serve.

The vegetable water may be saved and used in soups or stocks.

Baked Tomatoes

4 large tomatoes
Salt, pepper
1 oz (30 g) butter

1 Cut tomatoes in halves crossways.
2 Place in suitable dish cut sides uppermost.
3 Season and place a dab of butter on each.
4 Cover with plastic film.

Cook 3 to 4 minutes
depending on size. Turn
casserole a $\frac{1}{4}$ turn every
minute.

Aubergines Farcies Provençale (Stuffed Eggplant)

2 aubergines
2 tbsp olive oil
4 medium onions
4 large ripe tomatoes
1 crushed clove of garlic or squeeze of garlic powder
1 tsp chopped fresh parsley if available.
Salt, pepper
1 oz (30 g) Parmesan cheese
1½ oz (45 g) butter
Dried brown breadcrumbs

1 Cut aubergines in half lengthwise and with a
   sharp knife make criss-cross slits on the open
   flesh. Sprinkle with salt and place upside down
   for $\frac{1}{2}$ to 1 hour for moisture to come out. Rinse.
2 Place oil in a suitable casserole with drained
   aubergines. Cover.

Cook 3 minutes. Turn
dish $\frac{1}{2}$ turn after 1½
minutes.

3 Remove from oven and scoop out aubergine
   "meat". Set shells aside.

4 Place 1 oz (30 g) butter in the same casserole
and add onions, well chopped.   *Cook 4 minutes.*
5 Skin tomatoes and mix with onions and chopped
aubergine meat. Add seasoning, parsley and
garlic. Cover.   *Cook 3 minutes.*
6 Carefully pack stuffing into shells and replace
in casserole.
7 Sprinkle with Parmesan cheese and breadcrumbs
and a dab of the remaining ½ oz (15 g) butter.   *Cook 2 minutes
                                                 uncovered.*

Mushroom and Aubergine Quiche

4 oz (110 g) mushrooms   Salt, pepper
1 medium aubergine   1 oz (30 g) grated cheese
1 medium onion   4 tbsp olive oil
2 eggs   6-in pastry case
¼ pt (150 ml) milk

1 Chop mushrooms and onions and diced
skinned aubergine.
2 Place in a suitable casserole with oil, salt and
pepper.   *Cook 6 minutes,
                                                 stirring every 2
                                                 minutes.*
3 Beat eggs and milk together and stir into
mixture.
4 Pour mixture into pastry case.   *Cook 5 minutes,
                                                 turning dish every
                                                 1½ minutes.*
5 Sprinkle with grated cheese.
6 Serve hot or cold.

The pastry case may be made in the oven but I must emphasize
that the colour will be pale and the taste and texture will not be as
good as conventionally prepared pastry.

Stuffed Onions

2 large Spanish onions   Salt, pepper
1 slice of bread with crusts removed   1 oz (30 g) freshly minced beef
½ oz (15 g) margarine   1 tsp Worcestershire sauce
½ beaten egg   ¼ tsp ground coriander

1   Place onions in a suitable container.   *Cook 6 minutes.*
2   Remove centres of onion with a spoon or a
    grapefruit knife to make large cavities.
3   Chop onion centres and reserve.
4   Soak bread in egg and mash when soft enough.
5   Mash in margarine. Add salt, pepper, beef,
    sauce, spice and chopped onion.
6   Mix all the ingredients well together. Taste.
7   Fill onions with stuffing, pressing in firmly.
    Place a knob of butter on top.
8   Cover with paper.   *Cook 4 minutes,*
                                                              turning dish ½ turn
                                                              after 2 minutes.

Surplus stuffing should be rolled into balls and placed around the onions to be cooked at the same time.

Stuffed Peppers

2 small red peppers
2 oz (60 g) cooked rice
1 oz (30 g) seedless raisins
½ oz (15 g) chopped walnuts
Pinch of parsley
½ oz (15 g) butter
½ beaten egg
¼ tsp salt
¼ tsp ground nutmeg

1   Bring a pan half full of water to the boil on
    hob. Place the peppers in it. Reduce to simmer-
    ing point.   *3 minutes.*
2   Drain peppers, remove core and wash away
    seeds.
3   Prepare stuffing. Mix all other ingredients
    together.
4   Fill peppers with stuffing.
5   Brush outside of peppers with a little olive oil
    and place in a suitable dish that just fits.
6   Cover with a lid and cook for   *4 minutes, turning*
                                                              after 2 minutes.

Vegetarians would enjoy this light supper dish. I have chosen red peppers (capsicums) as they are more mellow than the green and blend well with the fruity filling. As accompaniment serve a green salad with a French dressing.

Patates Parmigiani

1 lb (450 g) washed and peeled potatoes
6 oz (170 g) grated Parmesan cheese
1 small onion
$\frac{1}{4}$ pt (150 ml) milk
1 can condensed cream of chicken soup
Pepper

1 Peel and finely chop onion. Slice the potatoes
   thinly.
2 Put layers of potato, onion and cheese in
   suitable casserole, beginning and finishing with
   potato.
3 Blend soup with milk and season with pepper.
4 Pour soup mixture over potatoes.

*Cook for 15 minutes.
turn dish $\frac{1}{4}$ turn every
3 minutes.*

For vegetarians use mushroom soup.
Serve as a vegetable or light supper dish.

Ratatouille

$\frac{1}{2}$ lb (230 g) courgettes
$\frac{1}{2}$ lb (230 g) aubergines
1 lb (450 g) onions
1 lb (450 g) tomatoes
2 green peppers
2 tbsp oil
Salt, pepper

1 Remove top and tail of aubergines. Slice thinly
   and sprinkle with salt.
2 Slice onions thinly.
3 Skin and quarter tomatoes.
4 Top and tail courgettes and cut into 1-in
   lengths.
5 Remove core of green peppers and rinse out
   any remaining seeds.
6 Thinly slice green peppers.
7 Place oil in suitable casserole with onions,
   green peppers, salt and pepper.

*Cook 10 minutes,
stirring after 5
minutes.*

8 Add courgettes.

Cook 10 minutes, stirring after 5 minutes.

9 Add tomatoes.
10 Rinse aubergines under cold water. Drain well.
11 Add aubergines to casserole.

Cook 10 minutes.

Aubergines, otherwise known as egg plants, are salted, rested and then rinsed for most recipes. The salt is to draw out the bitter juices and the method is called "dégorger".

Dégorger

To skin tomatoes, plunge into nearly boiling water for a few moments, and then dip in cold water. The skins will then come away easily.

Summer Casserole

4 oz (110 g) carrots
2 medium onions
½ lb (230 g) courgettes
4 oz (110 g) sliced green beans
Salt, pepper

Pinch of mixed herbs
¼ pt (150 ml) boiling water
½ chicken stock cube
4 oz (110 g) grated cheese

1 Prepare vegetables. Peel, scrape and thinly
  slice carrots. Top and tail courgettes and cut into
  $\frac{1}{2}$-in slices. Slice onions thinly, top and tail
  beans, remove strings and slice thinly.
2 Layer vegetables in suitable casserole, seasoning
  between the layers.
3 Add herbs to $\frac{1}{4}$ pt (150 ml) boiling water, add
  stock cube, dissolve and pour over vegetables.
4 Cover.   *Cook for 15 minutes,*
                                                     turning $\frac{1}{4}$ turn each five
                                                     minutes.

5 Top with grated cheese and brown under a pre-
  heated grill.

Serve as a supper dish or as a vegetable with steak or Wiener
schnitzel.

Microwave Fried Onions

1 large onion
2 tbsp cooking oil

1 Cut the onion in thin slices.
2 Place in suitable casserole with oil.
3 Cook until brown.   *Cook 10 minutes*
                                                     approx. Stir occasionally.

12 Egg and Cheese Dishes

When making sandwiches containing egg, it is wise to have the bottom slice of the bread thicker than the top one, when it will be possible to make an indentation in the centre with a spoon for the egg to rest in. You may otherwise find that the egg tends to slip out of the sandwich.

The timbale au fromage is only one example of this type of thickened egg/milk mixture, which also lends itself to a wide variety of flan fillings, the most well known being Quiche Lorraine. The timbale given here is not set in pastry and may be more attractive to those on a diet.

Omelettes have been omitted as I have not found them to be palatable enough cooked in the microwave, but omelettes re-heat well and can be previously prepared by conventional means and provided they are slightly undercooked can be dished on to individual suitable plates for rapid re-heating in the oven. This is a great time-saver when cooking for numbers.

For those wishing to boil eggs the answer is, yes it can be done — and no, they are not very good. Place the egg in a suitable egg-cup and tap on the top to crack the shell. Make a small hole in the shell with a skewer and cover with a small piece of paper. Place a glass of water in the back of the oven, to slow the cooking time. Now cook the egg for $\frac{1}{2}$ minute. Rest the egg for 2 minutes before eating as it will continue cooking after removal from the oven.

Bacon and egg

2 rashers of bacon   2 eggs

1   Place bacon on a sheet of kitchen paper on a

suitable plate. Cover with a sheet of kitchen
paper.   *Cook 2 minutes*
2 Remove paper from underneath bacon. This will
   have absorbed surplus fat.
3 Break 2 eggs on to plate with bacon. Cover
   with greaseproof paper.   *Cook $\frac{1}{2}$ minute.*
4 Switch off oven for a few seconds to "rest"
   eggs. Then   *Cook $\frac{1}{2}$ minute*
5 Rest again. Eggs are cooked when whites just
   begin to set. They continue cooking after
   removal from microwave oven.
6 Remove paper and serve.

Although it is said to be inadvisable to cook shelled, unbroken
eggs in the microwave oven, I have found that this is possible if
they are cooked with another food and rested during the cooking
period. However, it is advisable to cover during cooking, to save
a mess if they do explode.

Allow approximately 1 minute per rasher of bacon.

Eggs Aurore

4 hard-boiled eggs $\frac{1}{2}$ tsp finely chopped parsley
$\frac{1}{8}$ pt ($\frac{1}{4}$ lit) sauce aurore

1 Cut 3 freshly cooked hard-boiled eggs in even
   slices, preferably using an egg-slicer.
2 Sieve yolk of 4th egg and chop white finely.
   Reserve.
3 Prepare sauce.
4 Place a thin layer of sauce on base of dish.
5 Arrange slices of egg overlapping on top.
6 Coat evenly with sauce while nearly boiling.
7 Decorate with remaining egg, placing white in
   the centre and yolk around the edge of the dish.
8 Sprinkle chopped egg-white with parsley.

Sauce aurore

1 slice onion   2 oz (60 g) butter
2 blades mace   1 oz (30 g) flour
1 bayleaf   Salt, pepper
3 to 4 white peppercorns   3 oz (90 g) can tomato purée
$\frac{1}{2}$ pt ($\frac{1}{4}$ lit) milk

1 Heat milk in suitable jug with onion, mace, bayleaf and peppercorns.	*Cook 2 minutes.*
2 Remove from oven and set aside covered to infuse.	*20 to 30 minutes.*
3 Strain milk into a jug. Throw away vegetables and herbs.	
4 Melt 1 oz (30 g) butter in suitable casserole.	*Cook 1 minute.*
5 Blend in flour.	*Cook $\frac{1}{2}$ minute.*
6 Add milk carefully and stir well, season to taste.	*Cook to thicken 3 minutes approx., stirring every minute.*
7 Add tomato purée and beat in additional 1 oz (30 g) butter. Season to taste.	*Cook to bring back to boil, 1 to 2 minutes.*

Hot Egg and Bacon Sandwich

2 medium-thickness slices of bread   1 slice of bacon, with rind removed.
1 egg

1 Remove crusts from bread.	
2 Place 1 slice of bread on suitable plate.	
3 Break egg on to bread and cover with bacon.	
4 Cover with a second slice of bread and press down lightly.	*Cook $2\frac{1}{2}$ minutes.*

Leave a few moments to cool before eating.

The bacon fat will seep into the top slice of bread, giving added flavour.

A knife and fork for eating this one, please.

Hot Fried Egg Sandwich

2 medium-thickness slices of buttered bread   Salt, pepper
1 egg

1 Remove crusts from bread.	
2 Place one slice on a suitable plate.	
3 Break egg on to buttered bread. Season.	
4 Lightly press second slice of bread on top.	*Cook $1\frac{1}{2}$ minutes approx.*

Leave a few moments before eating, as this is very, very, hot.
Eggs are inclined to burst in the oven, but since this will happen within the sandwich it does not matter.

Scotch Woodcock

2 eggs
1 oz (30 g) butter
1 tbsp milk
½ tsp salt
Pinch of pepper
2 tsp anchovy essence ⎫
½ oz (15 g) butter ⎬ Blended together.
Paprika ⎭
4 anchovies
2 tsp capers
2 slices of toast

1 Cream butter, anchovy essence and paprika.
2 Make toast. Remove crusts. Cut each piece in half.
3 Spread with anchovy butter.
4 Chop capers.
5 Beat eggs. Add milk and salt and pepper.
6 Place butter in a suitable dish in the oven. *Melt 1 minute.*
7 Pour egg mixture into dish. *Cook 1½ to 2½ minutes, stirring every ½ minute.*

8 Pile egg mixture on to toast and garnish with anchovies and chopped capers.

Serve hot, as an after-dinner savoury, to those who do not enjoy a dessert or as a light supper dish.
Enough for 2.

Scrambled Eggs

2 standard eggs per person.   ¼ oz (10 g) butter
2 tbsp milk   Salt, pepper

1 Place butter in glass dish. *Melt 5 seconds.*
2 Break eggs into bowl with milk and salt and pepper and beat lightly.

3 Pour mixture into suitable dish.   *Cook 2 minutes, stirring*
                                                    every ½ minute.

Eggs continue cooking after removal from oven. Therefore they should be taken from the oven as soon as the mixture is set.

Slimmers' Cheese Snack (186 calories)

2 starch-reduced crispbreads.   1½ oz (45 g) Edam cheese

1 Place biscuits closely side by side on suitable
   plate.
2 Cover with thinly sliced Edam cheese.   *Cook 1½ minutes until*
                                                    cheese melts

N.B. Edam or Gouda cheese is better than Cheddar for this, as it has less calories per ounce (Edam or Gouda 88 calories per oz/per 30 g; Cheddar 120 per oz/per 30 g).

To make this dish more attractive, cook and serve with two thin slices of raw tomato on top.

Timbale au Fromage

2 standard eggs   3 oz (90 g) grated cheese
¼ pt (150 ml) milk   2 oz (60 g) canned cut green beans
4 oz (110 g) ham, chopped   Salt, pepper

1 Heat milk in a glass jug in oven.   *Cook 1 minute.*
2 Beat eggs and seasoning and add hot milk (not
   boiling)
3 Stir in cheese, ham and drained beans.
4 Place ½ pt (¼ lit) boiling water in a suitable dish
   in the oven.
5 Stand timbale dish in centre and cook until
   mixture begins to bubble.   *4½ minutes approx.*

This is a good choice for anyone on a high-protein diet.

This quantity will produce 3 portions in individual soufflé dishes.

13 Desserts: Fruits, Puddings and Jellies

A wide variety of sweets and puddings may be prepared either partially or wholly by microwave cookery.

Crumble mixture similar to shortcrust pastry, but with the binding agent omitted, is successfully used on any fruit base. Two versions of apple crumble are given but rhubarb, plums, apricots and canned fruits or canned pie fillings are among other suitable foundation fruits.

For crèmes caramel, brûlées and baked custards the ingredients listed in your usual recipe book should be used. Merely follow the method of cooking described in this chapter. To vary the few recipes in this book for custards, leave out the caramel base and substitute your own ones.

Gelatine dissolves easily and efficiently by the microwave method. For the more adventurous, follow the described method when preparing charlotte russe, bavarois, and creams.

Gelatine, which is a protein, is used for bulk in foods for those on diabetic, gastric or slimming diets, and is inexpensive.

Pear Hélène

4 canned pear halves
1 small block of vanilla ice cream
$\frac{1}{4}$ pt (150 ml) cold chocolate sauce
$\frac{1}{2}$ oz (15 g) mixed chopped nuts

1 Cut ice cream in two pieces and sandwich between pear halves.
2 Pour sauce over and top with nuts.

Pear Hélène

Bananas in Orange and Lemon Syrup

6 under-ripe bananas
1 oz (30 g) butter
4 tbsp castor sugar

Juice of $\frac{1}{2}$ a lemon
Juice of 1 orange
Few drops of Grand Marnier if liked

1 Skin bananas and cut in half lengthwise.
2 Place butter in suitable serving dish, melt in
   oven.   *Cook 20 seconds.*
3 Put cut bananas in dish.   *Cook 1$\frac{1}{2}$ minutes,*
                                                              turning dish and basting
                                                              bananas every $\frac{1}{2}$
                                                              minute.

4 Squeeze juices of fruit into a basin and blend
   with the sugar. Add liqueur if liked. Pour over
   bananas.   *Cook 15 seconds.*

Serve hot.

This interesting dessert will serve 4 people and is suitable for a special dinner party.

The bananas should be covered with a sheet of greaseproof paper during the whole of the cooking process.

Stewed Dried Fruits

Stewed Prunes

$\frac{1}{2}$ lb (230 g) prunes
1 oz (30 g) sugar

Water

1 Place prunes in suitable dish. Just cover with
   water and leave to soak for 2 hours.
2 Add sugar.   *Cook 5 minutes,*
                                                 stirring occasionally.

Prunes are good cooked in cold strained tea instead of water.

Stewed Apricots

½ lb (230 g) apricots   Water

1 Cover fruit with water in a suitable container
   and leave to soak for 2 hours.
2 Place in oven.   *Cook for 5 minutes,*
                                                 stirring occasionally.

Stewed figs

1 lb (450 g) figs   Water
1 oz (30 g) sugar

1 Place figs in suitable container. Just cover with
   water and leave to soak for 2 hours.
2 Add sugar.   *Cook for 10 minutes,*
                                                 stirring occasionally.

Stewed Dried Apples

½ lb (230 g) apple rings   1 oz (30 g) sugar
2 tsp lemon juice   Water

1 Place apple rings in a suitable container and
   just cover with water and lemon juice.
2 Leave to soak for 2 hours.
3 Add sugar.   *Cook for 5 minutes,*
                                                 stirring occasionally.

Upside-Down Pineapple Pudding

1 oz (30 g) soft brown sugar   *Cake mixture*
1 oz (30 g) margarine   2 oz (60 g) castor sugar
Small can of pineapple, drained   1 egg
A few glacé cherries   2 oz (60 g) self-raising flour
2 oz (60 g) margarine   7-in round glass cake-dish

1 Line or grease dish.
2 Cream brown sugar and 1 oz (30 g) margarine.
3 Spread over base and around sides of dish.

4 Arrange fruit on base. Glacé cherries should have the smooth side facing the dish.

5 Prepare cake mixture by the creaming method: i.e. cream margarine and sugar together until light and creamy. Add 1 tsp of flour, followed by the beaten egg, and then the remainder of the flour.

6 Place creamed mixture on top of the fruit.

Cook 6 minutes, turning dish a $\frac{1}{4}$ turn every $1\frac{1}{2}$ minutes.

7 Turn out on to a hot dish. Serve immediately or re-heat when needed for $\frac{1}{2}$ minute.

This attractive and economical sweet can be varied by using other fruits such as apricots, peaches or mandarin oranges.

Soft red fruits such as strawberries or raspberries are not suitable as the colour runs and the fruit goes mushy.

Baked Apples

2 cooking apples (about 6 oz (170 g) each)
2 tbsp water

$\frac{1}{2}$ oz (15 g) raisins
2 tsp demerara sugar

1 Wash and core the apples leaving them whole and unskinned.

2 Using a sharp knife score a spiral around the apple from top to base.

3 Place apples in a suitable container with water.

4 Mix raisins and sugar together and use to stuff cavities in the apples.

5 Cover with greaseproof paper.

Cook 3 to 4 minutes until tender.

Cooking time will vary with the size and shape of the apples.

Stewed Rhubarb

1 lb (450 g) rhubarb
2 tbsp cold tea

2 oz to 4 oz (60 g to 110 g) sugar

1 Wash, top and tail rhubarb.

2 Cut into $\frac{1}{2}$-in slices.

3 Place in suitable dish with cold tea and sugar.

4 Cover with paper.   *Cook 7 to 10 minutes,*
                       stirring occasionally.

Since rhubarb is an ideal slimmer's dessert the sugar may be omitted and 16 drops of artificial liquid sweetener added *after* cooking.

Orange Rhubarb Whip

1 lb (450 g) rhubarb   2 oz to 3 oz (60 g to 90 g) sugar
Grated rind and juice of 1 orange   2 egg whites.

1 Wash, top and tail the rhubarb and cut into
   $\frac{1}{2}$-in slices.
2 Place in suitable casserole with orange rind,
   juice, sugar and cover with paper.   *Cook 6 minutes,*
                                         stirring every 2
                                         minutes.
3 Liquidize or press through a sieve.
4 Leave to cool.
5 Whisk egg whites until stiff.
6 Carefully fold into purée.
7 Turn into individual glasses and serve
   immediately.

Serve with ice-cream wafers.
Use left-over egg yolks for thickening sauces, enriching milk puddings or for making mayonnaise.

Apricot and Apple Dessert

$\frac{1}{2}$ lb (230 g) dried apricots   Sugar to taste
Rind and juice of $\frac{1}{2}$ lemon   Whites of 2 to 3 eggs
2 medium-sized cooking apples   1 oz (30 g) chocolate drops
2 tbsp water

1 Cover apricots with cold water and soak for 2
   hours, drain.
2 Peel, core and slice apples and place in suitable
   casserole with apricots, lemon juice, grated
   lemon rind and 2 tbsp water.   *Cook 10 minutes,*
                                   stirring every 3
                                   minutes.

3 Liquidize or rub through a sieve. Leave to cool.
Sweeten to taste.
4 Whisk egg whites stiffly. Add gradually to cold
purée, whisking all the time.
5 Pile into individual glasses.
6 Chill and decorate with chocolate drops round
edges of glasses.

Apple Crumble (1)

1 lb (450 g) Bramley cooking apples	1 tbsp water
1 oz (30 g) castor sugar	Squeeze of lemon juice

Crumble

4 oz (110 g) plain flour	1 oz (30 g) castor sugar
2 oz (60 g) margarine	Pinch of salt

1 Peel, core and slice apples thinly.
2 Place in suitable dish with 1 oz (30 g) sugar,
lemon juice and water.

*Cook 6 minutes,
stirring every
2 minutes.*

3 Place flour and salt in mixing bowl and rub in
margarine. Add sugar.
4 Turn mixture on to cooked apples and press
down firmly.

*Cook 4 minutes, turning
dish $\frac{1}{2}$ turn after
2 minutes.*

5 To obtain a brown finish place under a hot
grill.
6 Sprinkle with sugar before serving.

Use the crumble mixture as a topping for commercially prepared pie fillings.

Apple Crumble (2)

1 lb (450 g) cooking apples	1 to 2 tbsp marmalade
1 to 2 tbsp water	$\frac{1}{2}$ oz (15 g) butter
2 oz (60 g) castor sugar.	

Crumble

4 oz (110 g) plain flour	1 oz (30 g) castor sugar
2 oz (60 g) butter or margarine	

1 Peel, core and slice apples and place in suitable casserole with water and sugar.

Cook 6 minutes, stirring every 2 minutes.

2 Add marmalade and butter and mix well.
3 In mixing bowl, rub butter into flour until mixture resembles breadcrumbs. Stir in sugar.
4 Place topping on apple mixture and return to oven.

Cook 4 minutes, turning dish $\frac{1}{2}$ turn after 2 minutes.

5 To brown, if required, place under hot grill for a few minutes.

Fruit Sponge with Lemon Sauce

4 oz (110 g) self-raising flour
2 oz (60 g) margarine
2 oz (60 g) castor sugar

1 oz (30 g) raisins
1 standard egg
Milk to mix

Sauce

4 oz (110 g) castor sugar
Scant $\frac{1}{2}$ oz (15 g) cornflour
8 fl oz (250 ml) water
1 oz (30 g) butter or margarine

Grated rind of half a lemon
Juice of half a lemon
Pinch of salt

Prepare sauce first as the sponge, if left to cool, will go hard. This is quickly remedied by re-heating for 15 seconds.

Sauce

1 Blend sugar, cornflour and cold water to a smooth paste.

Cook in oven for 2 minutes, stirring every $\frac{1}{2}$ minute.

2 Remove from oven and add remaining ingredients.

Sponge

1 Sieve flour into bowl.
2 Rub in fat.
3 Add dry ingredients.
4 Add beaten egg.
5 Mix to dropping consistency with a little milk, using metal spoon.

6 Grease pudding basin and add mixture.

Cook for 4 minutes approx. in centre of oven.

Turn on to a hot dish, pour over sauce and serve immediately. Use a 1-lb boilable pudding basin to cook this dessert. Serves 4.

Fresh Ginger Peach

3 peaches
3 tsp ginger jam

3 maraschino cherries
Fresh whipped cream

1 Wash the peaches but do not skin.
2 Halve the peaches, leaving stalk end uppermost. Remove stalks. Remove stones.
3 Place 1 tsp of ginger jam in cavity of lower half.
4 Replace top half of peach.
5 Place a maraschino cherry on top.
6 Stand in suitable dish.

Cook 1 minute per peach, i.e. 3 minutes for 3 peaches, cooked together.

7 Pipe cream round individual dessert plates and stand peach in centre.

These can only be cooked by the microwave method, as the peaches remain fresh and firm but the jam inside is hot.

Take care not to overcook, as the mouth could be burned by the jam.

Individual Fruit Charlottes

2 oz (60 g) shredded suet
4 oz (110 g) fresh white breadcrumbs
2 oz (60 g) demerara sugar

$\frac{1}{2}$ tsp ground nutmeg
Small tin pitted red cherries
1 cooking apple

4 individual soufflé dishes

1 Mix together suet, breadcrumbs, sugar and nutmeg.

2 Place a layer in base of each greased dish.
3 Drain and stone cherries and place 3 or 4 on
   top of charlotte mixture.
4 Add another layer of charlotte mixture.
5 Peel and core and thinly slice apple and place
   a layer of slices on mixture. Put two or three
   tsp cherry juice on top of the fruit.
6 Spread remaining mixture on top and press
   well down.
7 Place the 4 dishes on oven glass base, evenly
   placed round the centre.   *Cook 4 minutes,*
                                                      turning each dish after
                                                      2 minutes.

8 Flash charlottes under heated grill to brown
   tops.

Serve hot with custard, cream or ice cream.

Norwegian Cream

3 tbsp apricot jam $\frac{3}{4}$ pt (400 ml) milk
3 large eggs   3 tbsp whipped cream
1$\frac{1}{2}$ dessertspoonfuls sugar   Chocolate caraque or bar of chocolate flake
$\frac{1}{2}$ tsp vanilla essence.

1 Divide jam and spread in bases of 4 $\frac{1}{4}$-pt ($\frac{1}{8}$-lit.)
   soufflé dishes.
2 Warm milk in oven until hot but not boiling.   *Approx. 2 minutes.*
3 Break eggs and place 2 whole eggs and one
   yolk into a bowl. Beat lightly.
4 Add sugar, milk and vanilla essence.
5 Strain to remove threads from eggs.
6 Pour mixture evenly into dishes.
7 Place dishes in a glass dish containing $\frac{1}{2}$ pt
   ($\frac{1}{4}$ lit) of boiling water.   *Cook until cream*
                                                      begins to bubble —
                                                      4$\frac{1}{2}$ to 5 minutes.

8 Leave until cool.
9 Whip remaining egg white stiffly and fold into
   cream.
10 Pile on to creams and top with caraque or
   crumbled chocolate flake.

Serve with meringuettes.
If preferred cook in a 1-pt ($\frac{1}{2}$-lit) soufflé dish for 4$\frac{1}{2}$ to 5
minutes.

Use any flavour jam as a base.

To make chocolate caraque — melt a bar of plain chocolate and spread mixture thinly on a cold surface (use a formica surface only if it is already scratched). Using a long sharp knife, draw across the chocolate at a slight angle to form curls. There is a knack in doing this and it will be necessary to practise.

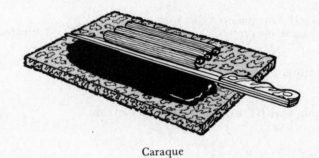

Caraque

Crème Caramel

Caramel	2 oz (60 g) loaf sugar
	2 tbsp water
Custard	4 large eggs
	$\frac{1}{2}$ oz to 1 oz (15 to 30 g) castor sugar
	1 pt ($\frac{1}{2}$ lit) milk
	Vanilla essence

4 soufflé dishes.

1 Prepare caramel on conventional hob. Dissolve sugar in water slowly until there are no crystals.
2 Raise heat and allow mixture to boil until it is dark brown in colour. Stay with it — IT MUST NOT BURN!
3 Pour into suitable dishes to coat bases. Leave to set.
4 Warm milk in oven till it is hot but not boiling.   *2 minutes approx.*
5 Break eggs into mixing bowl and beat lightly.
6 Add sugar, milk and vanilla essence.
7 Strain to remove threads from eggs.
8 Pour mixture on to caramel in the individual dishes.

9   Place dishes in a glass dish containing $\frac{1}{2}$ pt
    ($\frac{1}{4}$ lit) of boiling water.

*Cook until custards
begin to bubble —
$4\frac{1}{2}$ to 5 minutes.*

The custards will continue cooking after removal from the oven. Timing is approximate. Overcooking will tend to scramble the mixture.

Should you accidentally burn the syrup, switch off heat, pour boiling or very hot water into the pan. (Do not use cold water as the syrup will spit.) Throw syrup away. REMEMBER SUGAR BURNS ARE VERY PAINFUL.

Milk Jellies

1   Place jelly in 1 pt ($\frac{1}{2}$ lit) jug with $\frac{1}{4}$ pt ($\frac{1}{8}$ lit)
    water.

*Cook to dissolve —
$1\frac{1}{2}$ minutes.*

2   Stir. Leave to cool.
3   Make up to 1 pt ($\frac{1}{2}$ lit) with cold milk (approx.
    $\frac{1}{2}$ pt ($\frac{1}{4}$ lit).
4   Stir and place in jelly mould to set.

Serve milk jellies to children who dislike drinking milk or to the elderly invalid whose diet needs to be enriched.

Packet Jellies

1   Place jelly in 1 pt ($\frac{1}{2}$ lit) jug with $\frac{1}{4}$ pt (150 ml)
    water

*Cook to dissolve —
$1\frac{1}{2}$ minutes.*

2   Stir. Add cold water to make up to 1 pt ($\frac{1}{2}$ lit)
3   Stir, and place in jelly mould to set.

For a children's party make a *three-layer jelly*.

1   Dissolve and make up 1st jelly as above.
2   Empty into mould and place in refrigerator to set.
3   Make up 2nd jelly and when nearly set turn into same mould, to form a 2nd layer. Leave to set.

4 Make up 3rd jelly and when nearly set pour
   into mould to form 3rd layer.

This will only be successful if the jellies are nearly set when forming layers.

Fruit Jellies

1 Place jelly in 1 pt ($\frac{1}{2}$ lit) jug with $\frac{1}{4}$ pt (150
   ml) water.

*Cook to dissolve —
1$\frac{1}{2}$ minutes.*

2 Stir. Add any chopped or sliced fruit.
3 Make up to 1 pt ($\frac{1}{2}$ lit) with cold water.
4 Leave to cool until jelly just begins to set.
5 Stir well to distribute the fruit.
6 Turn into a jelly mould and leave in refrigerator
   to set.

Jelly cannot be frozen but refrigeration hastens setting. Do not use pineapple as the acid in this fruit prevents the jelly from setting properly.

Jellies made from Gelatine and Fruit Juices

$\frac{1}{2}$ oz (15 g) powdered gelatine
$\frac{3}{4}$ pt (400 ml) fruit juice
2 tbsp water

1 Stir gelatine into 2 tbsp water in a suitable jug.   *Cook 1 minute.*
2 Stir and set aside to clear and cool.
3 Place $\frac{3}{4}$ pt (400 ml) fruit juice in a bowl and
   holding the gelatine mixture about 6 in above
   the bowl, pour it in, stirring well.
4 Place in a mould and leave to set.

Gelatine mixture and juices must be combined at an even temperature if a tough or stringy result is to be avoided. Pouring from a height allows the gelatine to cool.

Use $\frac{1}{2}$ oz (15 g) or 1 small packet of gelatine to set 1 pt ($\frac{1}{2}$ lit) liquid. In summer or in warm conditions slightly more gelatine will be required.

Chocolate Cornflour Cream

1 pt ($\frac{1}{2}$ lit) milk
2 oz (60 g) cornflour
1 heaped tbsp cocoa
1 oz (30 g) castor sugar
$\frac{1}{2}$ tsp vanilla essence
Whipped cream

1 Blend cornflour, sugar and cocoa in a suitable
   bowl with a little of the cold milk.
2 Stir in remainder of milk.
3 Add vanilla essence.

*Cook $4\frac{1}{2}$ minutes,
whisking every 1
minute.*

4 Pour into $4\frac{1}{4}$-pt (150-ml) dishes.
5 When cool top with a tsp of whipped cream.

When using this basic recipe to prepare other flavours omit the
cocoa and vanilla essence and use flavourings and colourings of
your choice.

14 Sauces, Icings, etc

White sauces based on a roux (an equal quantity of fat and flour cooked together) cook easily in the microwave oven. Always remember to stir frequently and to whisk vigorously after cooking to remove any remaining lumps.

White sauces may also be cooked, by the one-step method, placing cold liquid, flour and fat together in a casserole and following the same directions. The results are thinner using this method, and for this reason it should be used when sauces are to be set aside, or frozen before re-heating. Sauces tend to thicken when stored.

This basic sauce has endless possibilities, and once mastered can be put to many uses. Milk, fish stock or chicken stock are suitable liquids. Parsley, capers, mustard, cheese, chopped hard-boiled egg, anchovy essence, prawns are all useful as additions.

The proportions for a pouring sauce are 1 oz (30 g) flour, 1 oz (30 g) fat to 1 pt ($\frac{1}{2}$ lit) milk. Those for a coating sauce are 2 oz (60 g) flour, 2 oz (60 g) fat to 1 pt ($\frac{1}{2}$ lit) milk. To test for consistency dip a spoon into the mixture, remove it and the sauce should coat the back of it.

A superior sauce is made by the infusion of herbs in warm milk for $\frac{1}{2}$ hour; this milk should be substituted after straining for the milk mentioned in the previous recipes.

Cornflour blended with cold liquid, sweetened and brought to boiling point is utilized in the preparation of custards and blancmange. Heat the ingredients together until thick and stir thoroughly and frequently during and after cooking. Flavour with coffee, chocolate, vanilla or liqueur.

Emulsified sauces such as mayonnaise may be prepared with the help of the microwave oven, but not entirely cooked in it. The mayonnaise recipe I have devised varies from the accepted method but produces successful results without any possibility of curdling. Add capers, parsley and chopped gherkins for Tartare sauce. A little anchovy essence and mustard will change Tartare sauce into Rémoulade. Yoghourt, sour cream, curry powder, a crushed clove of garlic or a tablespoon of tomato purée may be added to the basic recipe for mayonnaise for use with fish, meats or salads.

Barbecue sauce (for recipe see Barbecued Spare Ribs, page 57) and Bolognese sauce (see Spaghetti alla Bolognese, page 67) are not thickened with flour but the method as stated should be followed.

Bread Sauce

1 1-in thick slice of bread from a large loaf
1 onion, sliced
1 blade of mace
1 bayleaf
2 cloves

4 peppercorns
$\frac{1}{2}$ pt ($\frac{1}{4}$ lit) milk
$\frac{1}{2}$ (15 g) margarine
Salt to taste

1 Put onion and spices in a large suitable casserole with the milk.

Cook to boiling point, 2 minutes.

2 Cover and leave to infuse.
3 Strain milk and return to casserole.
4 Remove crusts from bread and soak in the milk.
5 Mash.
6 Season. Stir in margarine.

30 minutes.

15 minutes.
Re-heat 2 minutes.

Bread sauce is served with roast chicken or roast turkey.

A large vessel must always be used when bringing milk to the boil as it rises rapidly.

Béchamel Sauce

1 shallot or small onion
Piece of carrot
Stick of celery (optional)
Blade of mace
$\frac{1}{2}$ bay leaf
4 cloves

12 white peppercorns
1 pt ($\frac{1}{2}$ lit) milk
2 oz (60 g) butter or margarine
2 oz (60 g) flour
Salt
2 tbsp cream

1 Cut vegetables into pieces.
2 Place in casserole with milk, peppercorns, cloves, mace and bayleaf.

3	Bring nearly to boiling point.	*Cook 3 minutes approx.*
4	Remove from oven and cover. Leave in a warm place for 15 to 30 minutes.	
5	Strain into a bowl. Throw away vegetables.	
6	Place butter in casserole and place in oven.	*Cook 1 minute to melt.*
7	Add flour and stir well.	*Cook $\frac{1}{2}$ minute.*
8	Blend in milk. Season to taste.	*Cook uncovered to thicken − 4 minutes, stirring every $\frac{1}{2}$ minute.*
9	Add cream.	

Béchamel is a superior white sauce giving added flavour as a result of the infusion. When straining be careful not to do so over a sink as the mistake is easily made of keeping the vegetables and discarding the milk.

Mushroom Sauce

1 oz (30 g) butter	Scant $\frac{1}{2}$ pt ($\frac{1}{4}$ lit) milk	Salt, pepper
1 oz (30 g) flour	$\frac{1}{4}$ lb (110 g) mushrooms	

1	Place butter in a glass dish to melt.	*$\frac{1}{2}$ minute.*
2	Add flour.	*Cook $\frac{1}{2}$ minute.*
3	Blend in milk.	*Cook 3 minutes, stirring every 1 minute.*
4	Remove stalks from mushrooms. Wash and slice.	
5	Add mushrooms to sauce. Season.	*Cook 3 minutes, stirring every 1 minute.*

This thick sauce makes a good filling for vol-au-vent cases.

Vol-au-vent case

Sauce Soubise (Onion Sauce)

2 large onions
$\frac{1}{4}$ pt (150 ml) stock or $\frac{1}{4}$ pt (150 ml) water and $\frac{1}{2}$ chicken stock cube.
$\frac{1}{2}$ pt ($\frac{1}{4}$ lit) Béchamel sauce
Salt, pepper
Pinch of sugar
1 tbsp double cream half whipped

1 Peel and cut onions into quarters. Place in
  suitable casserole with stock or water and
  stock cube. Cover.   *Cook 7 minutes.*
2 Remove onions and liquidize or chop finely.
3 Mix onions with Béchamel sauce. Add sugar.
4 Thin down with onion liquor to desired consistency.
5 Season to taste. Stir in cream.

This sauce may be served with any fish or meat dish but is
particularly good with lamb dishes.

Tomato Sauce

$\frac{1}{2}$ oz (15 g) butter
$\frac{1}{2}$ rasher bacon
1 small onion
1 small carrot
$\frac{1}{2}$ lb (230 g) tomatoes
1 tsp tomato paste (from a tube preferably)
$\frac{1}{4}$ pt (150 ml) stock or $\frac{1}{4}$ pt (150 ml) water and $\frac{1}{2}$ chicken stock cube
Salt, pepper
Pinch of sugar
1 tsp cornflour

1 Place butter in a suitable casserole with cut-up
  strips of bacon.   *Cook $\frac{1}{2}$ minute.*
2 Chop onion and slice carrot thinly. Add to
  bacon.   *Cook 3 minutes,*
                                                stirring every 1 minute.

3 Skin and slice tomatoes and add together with
  tomato paste, stock or water and stock cube,
  salt, pepper and sugar.   *Cook 3 minutes approx.*
                                                to bring to boil.
4 Skim if necessary.   *Cook for a further*
                                                2 minutes.

5 When the vegetables are soft enough liquidize or press through a sieve. Return to casserole.
6 Blend cornflour with a little cold water and add to the sauce.

Cook 3 minutes approx. to thicken.

7 Correct seasoning and consistency and use as required.

If this sauce is to be served with fish, substitute 2 anchovy fillets for the bacon and fish stock for the chicken stock.

Velouté Sauce

$\frac{1}{2}$ oz (15 g) butter
2 white peppercorns
A few parsley stalks
1 oz (30 g) mushroom stalks
Salt

$\frac{3}{4}$ oz (20 g) flour
$\frac{1}{2}$ pt ($\frac{1}{4}$ lit) water
$\frac{1}{2}$ chicken stock cube
Juice $\frac{1}{4}$ lemon
1 tbsp cream

1 Place butter in suitable casserole.   *Cook $\frac{1}{2}$ minute.*
2 Add peppercorns and mushroom stalks and parsley.   *Cook 1 minute.*
3 Stir in flour.   *Cook $\frac{1}{2}$ minute.*
4 Gradually add water and add stock cube.   *Cook to thicken 2 to 3 minutes, stirring every 1 minute.*
5 Add lemon juice and salt.   *Cook 2 minutes; stir after 1 minute.*
6 Liquidize or press through a sieve.
7 Re-heat in oven.   *1 minute.*
8 Add cream.

It is better to liquidize the sauce as mushroom stalks are stringy and hard to press through a sieve.

Mayonnaise

1 egg yolk
$\frac{1}{4}$ tsp dry mustard
$\frac{1}{4}$ tsp salt

Pepper
1 tbsp vinegar
$\frac{1}{4}$ pt (150 ml) olive oil

1 Mix vinegar, salt, pepper and mustard in a small suitable bowl.   *Cook 20 seconds.*

2 Place oil in a suitable jug.   *Cook 30 seconds.*
3 Place egg yolk in a mixing bowl and using a
  rotary beater or hand-whisk add vinegar mixture
  to egg yolk and beat for 1 minute.
4 Add oil in a steady stream, beating vigorously at
  the same time.

If the mayonnaise is too thick, stir in 1 tsp boiling water and 1 tsp of vinegar. If the mayonnaise is not thick enough up to *1 fluid oz (30 ml)* may be beaten in.

1 egg yolk will not absorb more than *6 fluid oz (180 ml)*.

Should the mixture curdle, which is highly unlikely, place 1 tsp made mustard and 1 tsp curdled mayonnaise in a warm bowl, beat together and then beat in the remaining curdled mayonnaise, spoon by spoon.

Chocolate Sauce

2 oz (60 g) castor sugar
$\frac{1}{4}$ pt (150 ml) water
2 oz (60 g) cooking or dessert chocolate
$\frac{1}{2}$ tsp instant coffee

$\frac{1}{4}$ tsp vanilla essence
1 tsp cornflour
1 tbsp milk

1 Mix sugar and water in a large suitable bowl.
  Leave 5 minutes. Stir well.
2 Place in oven and bring to boil.   *Cook 2 minutes.*
3 After boiling point is reached, Cool slightly. *Cook 1 minute.*
  Add coffee and broken chocolate.
4 Stir to melt.
5 Blend cornflour with milk and add to chocolate
  mixture. Stir, bring to boiling point to thicken. *Cook 1½ minutes*
                                                   approx.
6 Stir in vanilla essence.

Serve hot with vanilla ice cream, with ice cream topped with chopped nuts or cold with Pear Hélène, as this chocolate sauce is equally good hot or cold.

Custard Sauce

$\frac{1}{2}$ oz (15 g) sugar.
$\frac{1}{2}$ pt ($\frac{1}{4}$ lit) milk.
1 level tbsp custard powder OR 1 level tbsp cornflour and $\frac{1}{2}$ tsp vanilla essence.
$\frac{1}{4}$ oz (10 g) butter.

1 Place custard powder in a basin and gradually
   blend in milk.
2 Stir in sugar.
3 Place in oven.   *Cook 3 minutes,*
                                         stirring every minute.
4 Remove from oven and add a dot of butter.

Although the butter will help to prevent a skin from forming, the
sauce should be covered with a damp disc of greaseproof paper,
wet side down.

Sauces to be served separately can be prepared in a suitable
serving jug.

Crème Pâtissière (Confectioners' Custard)

$1\frac{1}{2}$ gills (225 ml) ($7\frac{1}{2}$ fluid oz) milk $1\frac{1}{2}$ oz (45 g) sugar
1 egg yolk $\frac{1}{2}$ tsp vanilla essence or 1 tsp rum
2 oz (60 g) unsalted butter   1 tbsp cream
$1\frac{1}{2}$ oz (45 g) flour

1 Mix flour with nearly all the cold milk.
2 Add sugar and butter.   *Cook $1\frac{1}{2}$ minutes*
                                         until thick; stir every
                                         $\frac{1}{2}$ minute.
3 Beat thoroughly with a fork to disperse lumps.
4 Mix beaten egg yolk with remainder of milk
   and vanilla essence or rum.
5 Add to mixture and beat thoroughly.   *Cook $\frac{1}{2}$ minute.*
6 Add cream.
7 Press through a strainer to remove any lumps.
8 Cover with damp greaseproof paper wet side
   down until required.

A fork is preferable to a spoon when blending and beating.
This is the custard used in French pastries.
Use as a base in pastry cases and top with fruit.

Apricot Glaze

2 tbsp apricot jam   2 tbsp water

1 Place jam and water in suitable casserole in
   oven. Stir and cover.   *Cook $1\frac{1}{2}$ minutes.*

2 Strain to remove pieces of apricot.
3 Leave to cool. Store in a covered container in
   a refrigerator.

Apricot glaze must reach boiling point before using; if this is
not done it may go mouldy. This is particularly important when
using on a wedding or Christmas cake under marzipan, for these
cakes have to be kept for a long time.

Stock Syrup

$\frac{1}{2}$ lb (230 g) granulated sugar
$\frac{1}{4}$ pt (150 ml) water

1 Mix sugar with water in a suitable casserole.
2 Leave 1 hour.
3 Place in oven and bring to boil.   *Cook 2 to 3 minutes.*
                                                   Cover and boil for 2
                                                   more minutes.

Leave to cool and store in a covered container in the refrigerator.
Use as required.
Use stock syrup with fresh fruit salad or in any recipe where
syrup is required.

Glacé Icing

6 oz (170 g) icing sugar
2 tsp water
Colouring, flavouring

1 Sieve the icing sugar into a bowl.
2 Add 1 tsp water and blend.
3 Add remaining tsp water.
4 Add colouring and flavouring.

If the icing is too thin add more icing sugar.
A few drops of lemon juice in place of the 2nd tsp of water will
give a piquancy that will take away the very sweet taste.
For chocolate icing blend 2 tsp of cocoa with the water before
adding to the icing sugar.

Fudge Icing

2 tbsp milk
2 oz (60 g) unsalted butter or soft margarine
7 oz (200 g) icing sugar
Colour, flavouring

1 Place milk and butter in suitable bowl and
   melt.   *Cook 1½ minutes.*
2 Sieve icing sugar into mixture, beating well until
   smooth.
3 Add colouring and flavouring.

For chocolate icing dissolve 1 level tbsp cocoa with milk and margarine.

This icing quickly forms a crust. If it is not to be used immediately cover with damp greaseproof paper wet side down until required. Fudge icing may be gently re-heated in the oven before use.

15 Jams and Conserves

Only three recipes are in this section because the microwave method of preparing and cooking jam is the same whichever fruit you choose.

Fruit contains a substance known as pectin. Fruits which contain large amounts of pectin will set well, but those with only a little will have to have pectin added. The fruits in these recipes are high in pectin, as also are gooseberries, sour apples, blackcurrants and citrus fruits. Strawberries, raspberries and cherries, which contain very little pectin, will produce a better yield if they are cooked with a small quantity of fruit rich in pectin. Gooseberries or apples are suitable additives but instead of such fruits, lemon juice, tartaric acid or commercial pectin may be used.

Bitter oranges, grapefruit, limes and lemons are all suitable for marmalade, but the fruit will remain tough if it is not soaked for several hours before cooking. When tender, follow the microwave method.

Apricot Conserve

1 lb (450 g) fresh apricots
1 lb (450 g) sugar (preserving or castor)
$\frac{1}{4}$ pt (150 ml) water mixed with squeeze of lemon juice

1 Cut apricots in half and remove stones.
2 Crush 6 stones to remove kernels. Blanch kernels and add to apricots.
3 Place apricots in water and lemon juice in a suitable very large casserole.   *Cook 10 minutes.*
4 Stir in sugar. Leave 15 minutes to dissolve.
5 Place uncovered in oven.   *Cook 30 minutes approx.*

6　Test after 20 minutes. Thermometer reading
　　should be 220°F or 103°C or a drop on a cold
　　plate should wrinkle.
7　Remove from oven and pot in a hot jam-jar.

This makes 1½ lb conserve. It will keep unpotted in a refrigerator
for about 3 weeks.

If testing with a thermometer be sure to remove it before
continuing to cook, as metal will break the magnetron.

To blanch, place the kernels in a pan cover with cold water and
bring to boil. Strain immediately and remove skins.

Plum Jam

1 lb (450 g) plums or cherry plums　　¼ pt (150 ml) water
1 lb (450 g) castor sugar

1　Using a very very tall pot, stew the plums with
　　the water.　　　　　　　　　　　　　　　　*Cook 15 minutes.*
2　Remove from oven and stir in sugar. Leave until
　　sugar is dissolved, *approximately 15 minutes.*
3　Return to oven. Cook to bring to boil and con-
　　tinue boiling until setting point is reached. Use
　　flake or wrinkle test.　　　　　　　　　　*15 minutes approx.*
4　Remove from oven with oven gloves and place
　　on a heatproof surface to cool a little.
5　Remove plum stones.

Yield 1⅓ lb.

This freshly made jam has an excellent flavour. As the yield is
small there is no need to pot and seal. When cold keep covered in
refrigerator. Jam will keep at least two weeks.

Tests for setting point — a spoonful dropped on to a cold
saucer should wrinkle or when a wooden spoon is removed from
mixture a drop of jam should be seen to hang from the edge.

When cooking jam quite a lot of condensation will form
outside the oven. This is easily wiped after cooking is complete.

Redcurrant Jam

1 lb (450 g) red currants　　　　　　¼ pt (150 ml) water
1 lb (450 g) sugar

1 Wash and remove stalks from currants.
2 Place in large suitable bowl. *Cook 15 minutes.*
3 Add sugar, stir and set aside for 30 minutes.
4 Add ¼ pt (150 ml) water and stir well.
5 Cook until jam reaches 220°F (103°C), or test *About 20 minutes.*
  by dipping a wooden spoon into the jam; turn
  spoon until a drop of jam hangs on the edge —
  this is called the flake test.
6 Pot in the usual way.

This will produce 1¼ lb of jam, which will have a clear bright colour.

Although it is only practicable to make small quantities of jam in the oven, the speed and ease of preparation make it possible to produce a good conserve from whatever fruit is plentiful at the time. There is something especially attractive about newly prepared jams with their fresh fruit bouquet.

16 Cakes, Biscuits and Pastry

Cake making in the microwave oven is extremely fast. The best results are obtained when making large cakes. These should contain a good quantity of fat and whenever using recipes other than those given here substitute golden syrup for some of the sugar. Be sure that mixtures are on the loose side. Thick batter mixtures made by the melting method, such as ginger cake, stay moist and keep well.

Chocolate cake, ginger cake and fruit cake which contain dark ingredients need no embellishment, but light mixtures, such as Victoria sponges and Madeira cake, will not brown. This can be disguised by icing, covering with apricot glaze or marzipan, grated chocolate, sieved icing sugar, cinnamon, crumbled biscuits or browning under the grill.

The dark fruit cake recipe given is not dissimilar to Christmas cake mixture and could be marzipanned and royal-iced in 1 hour.

A cake is cooked when it is just dry in the centre on top. The cake will not be harmed when the oven door is opened to turn the dish. Cakes continue to cook after removal from the oven; over-cooking will cause cakes to become "biscuity" inside.

Stale cake may be refreshed by re-heating for $\frac{1}{2}$ minute in the microwave oven.

Biscuits will cook but not brown. Mixtures dropped in teaspoonsful on the lined oven base will be successful but rolled-out mixtures shaped with cutters will lose their shape. Should you wish to make biscuits from such a mixture it would be best to cook a sheet of rolled-out mixture and cut it into biscuits after cooking but while still hot.

Pastry should be rolled thinly and pricked well on the sides as well as the base. While not suggesting that the microwave oven is a good medium for pastrymaking, results will be better if water is omitted and beaten egg yolk or milk is substituted.

Suitable round dishes may be lined with plastic film, vegetable parchment or greased greaseproof paper.

To line a round dish cut a circle of parchment to fit the base. Cut a second oblong strip to fit the perimeter. Fold 1 inch under and then open out; using scissors cut to the fold at 1-inch intervals. It will be possible to curve this lining inside the edge of the dish. Place the circle of parchment or greaseproof paper (greased) in base of dish over the side lining.

The microwave oven cannot make toast but thick slices of bread can be turned into crunchy rusks in a minute or two.

Use your oven to help you to make cakes. It will soften or melt butter, or chocolate, warm milk for yeast mixtures and combine ingredients for basic syrup.

Apfel Strudel

1 12-in square of strudel pastry.
1 medium-sized cooking apple
1 oz (30 g) sultanas
1 oz (30 g) castor sugar
2 tsp cinnamon
2 oz (60 g) butter
$\frac{1}{2}$ oz (15 g) demerara sugar

1 Peel and core and chop apple into $\frac{1}{2}$-in dice.
2 Place butter in glass dish or saucer and melt in
   oven.   *$1\frac{1}{2}$ minutes.*
3 Brush pastry with butter. Sprinkle apple, sultanas,
   sugar and 1 tsp of cinnamon evenly over the
   surface.
4 Roll up like a Swiss roll but fold sides of
   pastry up over the mixture.

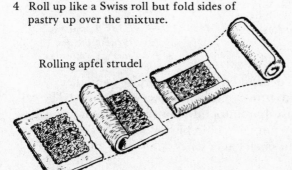

Rolling apfel strudel

5 Place in suitable dish that just fits it.
6 Pour remainder of butter over strudel.

*Cook 4 minutes,
turning the dish after
2 minutes.*

7 Sprinkle with demerara sugar and 1 tsp
cinnamon.
8 Brown quickly under a pre-heated grill if
desired.
9 Leave to cool 5 minutes before serving, as
sultanas become very hot during cooking.

Recipes for strudel pastry can be found in most cookery books, but for a small quantity it is simplest to buy it. Either purchase a small packet from a continental grocer or as "Filo" from a Greek store.

Chocolate Cake

4 oz (110 g) soft margarine
4 oz (110 g) castor sugar
2 standard eggs
4 oz (110 g) golden syrup

$1\frac{1}{2}$ oz (45 g) ground almonds
4 oz (110 g) self-raising flour
2 oz (60 g) cocoa
4 fluid oz (150 ml) milk

1 Cream margarine and sugar until light and
fluffy.
2 Beat eggs and add one at a time. Beat well.
3 Mix flour cocoa and ground almonds and
sieve on to mixture. Fold in.
4 Add milk.
5 Add golden syrup and stir.
6 Line a 2-pt (1-lit) glass dish.
7 Smooth mixture into this.

*Cook 6 minutes,
turning the dish
every $1\frac{1}{2}$ minutes.*

Cooking time will depend on the shape of the container chosen. Watch the mixture carefully as cakes burn easily. The cake is ready when it is just dry on top; do not test with your fingers as the mixture is very hot and could burn you.

Use this mixture in small paper cases, allowing $\frac{1}{2}$ minute per cake.

This cake may be iced with fudge or glacé icing.

Chocolate Malakoff Gâteau

$1\frac{1}{2}$ packets of sponge fingers
1 tbsp sherry or rum
3 oz (90 g) plain chocolate
6 oz (170 g) castor sugar
6 oz (170 g) butter
1 egg yolk

1 Line a 1-lb loaf-tin with plastic film, folding
   surplus to outside.

16   Lining a "cake-tin" with plastic film

N.B. The "tin" must be a non-metallic container.

2 Put chocolate in glass bowl and melt in oven.   *$1\frac{1}{2}$ minutes.*
3 Add butter to chocolate mixture.   *Cook 1 minute.*
4 Add sugar and stir.   *Cook $\frac{1}{2}$ minute.*
5 Add beaten egg yolk and mix thoroughly.
6 Place rum or sherry on a plate and dip sponge
   fingers in quickly.
7 Place the biscuits in base of tin, fitting in
   broken pieces where necessary.
8 Cover with a layer of chocolate sauce.
9 Continue alternating layers of biscuits and
   layers of sauce, finishing with sauce.
10 Cover with greaseproof paper and put a weight
   on top to prevent the biscuits from floating.
11 Refrigerate or freeze for 1 to 2 hours.
12 Turn out, remove paper and decorate with
   whipped cream rosettes and glacé cherries.

This will yield 12 servings as it is very rich. Undecorated it will
keep for several weeks in a freezer, but it is not happy if kept too
long in a warm atmosphere.

Fruit Cake

2 tsp baking powder
$\frac{1}{4}$ lb (110 g) plain flour
1 tsp mixed spice
5 oz (145 g) dried mixed fruit
1 oz (30 g) glacé cherries, washed and chopped
Pinch of salt
3 oz (90 g) dark brown sugar
3 tbsp milk
2 large eggs
3 oz (90 g) butter or soft margarine

1 Cream the butter or margarine with sugar until
   light and fluffy.
2 Add beaten eggs.
3 Add milk.
4 Add remaining ingredients and mix well.
5 The mixture should be of a soft dropping
   consistency, a little more milk being added if
   necessary.
6 Line a suitable container.

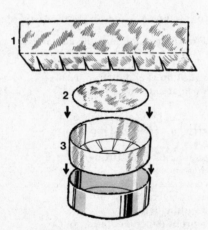

Lining a "cake-tin" with paper

1   Cut a piece of paper equal to the perimeter of the "tin" and of
similar depth plus 1 in. Fold up 1 in along the length of the paper, open
out and make cuts at 1-in intervals up to the fold.   2   Cut circle of
paper to fit base of tin.   3   Curve first piece of paper to form a circle
and fit inside. Put the second piece of paper inside, on the base.
N.B. The "tin" must be a non-metallic container.

7 Place mixture in dish making a depression in the middle.
8 Place in oven.

Cook for 6 minutes, turning dish a $\frac{1}{4}$ turn every $1\frac{1}{2}$ minutes.

When preparing cake mixtures for microwave cookery it is better to have the mixture too wet rather than too dry.

If you have an electric mixer place all the ingredients in together and beat for 2 to 3 minutes at a slow speed.

Ginger Cake

$\frac{1}{2}$ lb (230 g) flour
1 level tsp bicarbonate of soda
3 oz (90 g) margarine
2 oz (60 g) brown sugar
$1\frac{1}{2}$ level tsp ground ginger.

1 large egg
5 tbsp milk approx.
2 oz (60 g) crystallized ginger
6 oz (170 g) golden syrup

1 Place syrup, margarine and sugar in a suitable bowl.

Cook $1\frac{1}{2}$ minutes. Stir well.

2 Sieve flour, bicarbonate of soda and ground ginger into a mixing bowl.
3 Add beaten egg and 2 tbsp milk to syrup mixture.
4 Combine with flour mixture and beat well.
5 Add 3 more tbsp milk to make a thick batter consistency.
6 Chop ginger and mix in.
7 Pour into lined glass cake-dish (9-in diameter).

Cook $5\frac{1}{2}$ minutes, turning $\frac{1}{4}$ turn every $1\frac{1}{2}$ minutes.

This mixture may be cooked in individual paper cases, each requiring one minute.

4 cakes cooked at one time, placed close together on oven base, will take $3\frac{1}{2}$ minutes.

Lemon Cheesecake

6 oz (170 g) digestive biscuits ⎫
3 oz (90 g) margarine   ⎬ for base
Pinch of cinnamon   ⎭

2 large eggs	Grated rind and juice of 1 lemon
4 oz (110 g) castor sugar	$\frac{1}{8}$ pt (70 ml) double cream to decorate
14 oz (400 g) curd cheese	

1 Crush digestive biscuits.
2 Whisk eggs and sugar together until thick.
3 Add cheese, lemon rind and juice. Whisk.
4 Melt margarine in 10-in suitable round dish. *Cook 1½ minutes.*
5 Add crushed biscuits and cinnamon to margarine and mix together.
6 Press biscuit mixture into base and sides of the dish.
7 Spoon cheese mixture on top of the biscuits. Smooth with a palette knife.
8 Place in oven. *Cook 6 minutes; turn dish a ¼ turn every 1½ minutes.*
9 Leave to cool then put in a refrigerator until set and firm. *1 hour.*
10 Decorate with piped whipped cream.

Cheese cake is ready when just dry in the centre; cooking will continue while the cake is cooling.

To crush biscuits, place in a large polythene bag, lay flat and press with a rolling pin or an empty milk bottle.

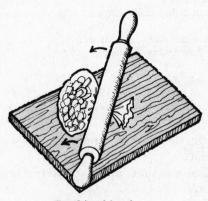

Crushing biscuits

Rum Baba

4 oz (110 g) strong or plain flour	3 to 4 tbsp milk
1 tbsp castor sugar	$\frac{1}{4}$ oz (10 g) yeast
2 standard eggs	2½ oz (75 g) butter or margarine

1 oz (30 g) currants
Apricot glaze
$\frac{1}{2}$ pt ($\frac{1}{4}$ lit) syrup ⎫
Juice $\frac{1}{2}$ lemon ⎬ or juice from canned fruit
2 tsps rum ⎭

1 Warm milk in jug in oven.   *Cook 20 seconds.*
2 Add yeast and blend together.
3 Add beaten egg.
4 Add sugar.
5 Beat liquid into sifted flour to make a batter.
   Beat for at least 5 minutes.
6 Cover bowl and leave to rise in a warm place for
   40 minutes.
7 Cut butter into small pats and beat with the
   currants into the batter.
8 Divide between 6 or 8 greased oven glass moulds
   ($\frac{1}{4}$-pt size).
9 Cover and leave until double in size.
10 Bake 3 at a time.   *Cook 2 minutes for*
                                           3 moulds.

11 Loosen sides with a knife and turn on to a dish.
12 Baste with hot syrup.
13 Glaze with apricot glaze.
14 Decorate with glacé cherries, angelica leaves and
   whipped cream when cool.

Truffles

6 oz (170 g) stale cake crumbs (fruit cake is ideal)
1 oz (30 g) butter
2 heaped tbsp apricot jam
1 oz (30 g) cocoa
1 oz (30 g) ground almonds
$\frac{1}{2}$ tsp vanilla essence
2 tsps rum
Chocolate vermicelli

1 Place butter in dish to melt.   *$\frac{1}{2}$ minute.*
2 Add jam and cocoa. Put in oven to melt.   *$\frac{1}{2}$ minute.*
3 Mix in vanilla essence, rum, ground almonds
   and cake crumbs.
4 Form into balls and roll in chocolate vermicelli.
5 Leave to cool in refrigerator.

    This is a useful way to use up left-over cake. Truffles can be
quickly prepared for unexpected guests.

Yoghourt Sponge Cake

6 oz (170 g) soft margarine
1 large egg
6 oz (170 g) self-raising flour
6 oz (170 g) castor sugar
2 cartons yoghourt (hazelnut is best, but natural sweetened may be used instead.
2 level tbsp cocoa
3 tbsp milk
3 oz (90 g) desiccated coconut.

1 Line a 9-in-diameter glass dish with plastic film.
2 Place margarine in a suitable dish in oven. *Melt 1½ minutes, stirring after ½ minute.*

3 Stir in sugar
4 Beat egg and add with one carton of yoghourt.
5 Sieve flour and fold in.
6 Turn mixture into prepared dish and spread evenly. *Cook 6 minutes, turning dish ¼ turn every 1½ minutes.*

7 Blend cocoa with milk and add second carton of yoghourt. Stir in coconut.
8 With scissors cut away any plastic film showing over the edge of the dish.
9 Spread cocoa mixture evenly over the cooked sponge and place under a pre-heated grill for *2 to 3 minutes to set.*
10 Sprinkle with castor sugar.
11 Leave for at least 10 minutes.

Serve hot with cream or custard, being careful not to cut through the plastic film, or leave until cold when the cake should be lifted gently from the dish and the plastic film removed.

This is an unusual mixture of sweet and sour flavours and could be served as a special occasion gâteau if topped with rosettes of freshly whipped cream and decorated with silver balls.

Meringuettes (biscuits)

1 egg white
2 oz (60 g) castor sugar
1 oz (30 g) flour
¼ tsp vanilla essence

1 oz (30 g) butter
2 oz (60 g) melted chocolate
Sheet of vegetable baking parchment

1 Melt butter in small glass.
  Set aside to cool.   *Cook 30 seconds.*
2 Beat egg white until thick and add sugar.
  Continue to beat until mixture is thick and
  holds a peak.
3 Add vanilla essence.
4 Fold in flour.
5 Add melted butter and mix lightly.
6 Cut a sheet of vegetable parchment to fit the
  base of the oven and place six teaspoonfuls of
  mixture on this well spread out.   *Cook ½ minute.*
7 Turn parchment round and continue cooking
  until biscuits are just turning brown.   *Cook ½ minute.*
8 Remove paper from oven, lift biscuits off with
  a fish slice or palette knife and leave to cool.
9 Melt chocolate, place on plain saucer and cook
  until it is seen to just soften on top.   *Cook 1½ minutes.*
10 Dip biscuits in chocolate at opposite edges and
   leave to set.

Dipping in chocolate

The biscuit being dipped into liquid chocolate is held with tongs.

These biscuits burn easily and the signs of browning are in fact
signs of burning, so they must be watched carefully. Ignore the
fact that the biscuits look unattractive. This will not be noticed
when the chocolate is on and the taste is delicious.

Parkin

6 oz (170 g) porridge oats   Grated rind of 1 lemon
2 oz (60 g) plain flour   1 tsp ground ginger

$\frac{1}{2}$ tsp bicarbonate of soda
2 oz (60 g) black treacle
2 oz (60 g) golden syrup

2 oz (60 g) margarine
2 tbsp milk

1 Place treacle, syrup and margarine in suitable jug or bowl.

Cook until melted – $1\frac{1}{2}$ minutes.

2 In another bowl mix oatmeal, flour, lemon rind and ginger.
3 Add syrup mixture to dry ingredients and mix well.
4 Mix milk and bicarbonate of soda and add to mixture. Beat well.
5 Line a suitable container with vegetable parchment or plastic film.
6 Turn mixture into container and press down evenly. It should be $\frac{3}{4}$ in thick. Mark portions with a knife.

Cook for 3 minutes, turning dish after $1\frac{1}{2}$ minutes.

7 Turn out, remove film and leave to cool.

Parkin will continue cooking after removal from the oven. It may not seem to be cooked when it is hot but overcooking will toughen it.

Shortbread with Wholemeal Flour

5 oz (140 g) unsalted butter
6 oz (170 g) wholemeal flour
2 oz (60 g) ground rice

1 oz (30 g) castor sugar
Pinch of salt

1 Sieve flour, ground rice and salt into a mixing bowl
2 Rub in butter until the mixture resembles breadcrumbs.
3 Stir in sugar.
4 Press mixture firmly into a suitable lined container.
5 Prick all over with a fork.

Cook $3\frac{1}{2}$ minutes, turning dish a $\frac{1}{4}$ turn every minute.

6 Mark portions with a knife.
7 Leave to cool, turn out and remove plastic film lining.

8 Sprinkle with sugar.

This shortbread is very quickly prepared and cooked. Store in an airtight tin.

Shortcrust Pastry

8 oz (230 g) plain flour   2 tbsp cold milk
4 oz (110 g) cooking fat

1 Rub fat into flour.
2 Add milk and mix to form a firm paste.
3 Roll out and use as desired.

When using for flan or patty cases make sure to prick the sides as well as the base thoroughly.

For a 6-in pie shell you will require pastry made from 4 oz (110 g) flour.

Prick, cook in oven for 4 minutes approx. turning a $\frac{1}{4}$ turn every minute.

17 Miscellaneous and Beverages

This chapter contains recipes that did not seem to fit into any of
the preceding ones. On the other hand some recipes which might
have been included in this chapter will be found in other sections of
the book. For example, you will find baked beans under Meat
and Poultry, as you may wish to cook sausages and baked beans to
make one dish. Similarly poppadums and chapatis, which are
accompaniments for curry, are grouped together, and stuffing is to
be found with poultry.

The re-constitution of dried vegetables is in this miscellaneous
section as I have tried to group this processed food together.
Barbecue, sweet and sour and bolognese sauces are also in the meat
and poultry chapter, but the re-constituted sauces follow here.

If you cannot find a component part of a recipe under a specific
heading, please refer to the index, which has been made as com-
prehensive as possible.

Any milk or water beverage may be quickly prepared in the
microwave oven. The great advantage is that it is easier to judge
the amount required and the liquid is heated in your drinking cup
or glass. A glass of water boils in two minutes and a teabag may
then be popped in, avoiding unnecessary waste of fuel by over-
filling a kettle. When re-heating pre-cooked coffee do not let it
boil or it will become bitter. Milk is inclined to boil over and must
be watched carefully, although a spill is easy to wipe away.

The microwave oven is very versatile in its uses. Try roasting
coffee beans or chestnuts (making sure the skins are cut through).
Make fudge or coconut ice. When you become accustomed to the
oven you will find it easy to adapt recipes from your favourite
cookery book and will be able to experiment and fill the gaps that
limited space in this volume inevitably leaves.

Reconstituting dried packet soups

Mix as directed on packet.
Normally this is 5 oz (145 g) to 1 pt (½ lit)
water.
Thin soups such as spring vegetable, chicken
noodle, etc., need to be placed in a suitable
casserole to cook until the vegetables are
tender.   *10 minutes approx.*

Thick soups should be cooked in a suitable
casserole until the soup thickens.   *4 minutes approx.,
                                                 stirring frequently.*

Re-constitute *dried sauce mixes* in the same way.

Freeze-dried Vegetables

1 oz (15 g) freeze-dried beans.   Salt
1 pt (½ lit) water

Place beans in suitable casserole with salted
water. Stir.   *Cook 6 minutes.*

Cook other freeze-dried vegetables similarly. Those obtainable
are cabbage, carrots, swedes, onions and peas.

Porridge

1 cup porridge oats   Salt or sugar to taste
3 cups water or 2 cups water and 1 cup milk

1 Place oats and water or oats and milk and
   water in a large suitable bowl.
2 Stir well.   *Cook 5 minutes,
                                                 stirring after 2 minutes.*

3 Allow to stand for a few minutes before
   serving.
4 Add salt or sugar to taste.

Hot Grapefruit Dubonnet

1 grapefruit
½ oz (15 g) dark brown sugar   1 tbsp Dubonnet
¼ oz (10 g) butter   2 maraschino cherries

1 Cut the grapefruit into halves crosswise.
2 Loosen segments with a grapefruit knife and remove centre core with scissors.
3 Sprinkle with sugar and dot with butter.
4 Place in a suitable casserole or individual cereal bowls. *Cook 2½ minutes.*
5 Pour Dubonnet over the grapefruit halves. Place a cherry in the centre of each and serve hot.

An unusual starter which can be prepared beforehand, ready to cook when guests are at the table.

Coffee

1 pt (½ lit) water   4 level tbsp medium-ground coffee

1 Place water in large suitable jug. *Bring to boil, 5 minutes.*
2 Remove from oven while bubbling, add coffee and stir with a wooden spoon.
3 Leave to settle a few minutes before pouring.

Never stir coffee with a metal spoon as it will spoil the flavour.

Turkish coffee

1 pt (½ lit) water
2 heaped dessertspoonsful castor sugar
3 heaped dessertspoonsful pulverized fresh coffee

1 Place water in large suitable casserole and stir in sugar and coffee.	*Cook to boiling point, 4½ minutes approx.*
2 Rest.	*5 minutes.*
	Cook to boiling point, 4½ minutes.
3 Rest.	*5 minutes.*
Stir.	*Cook to boiling point, 1½ minutes.*
4 Rest.	*5 minutes.*
Stir.	*Cook to boiling point, 1½ minutes.*
5 Do not stir again. Rest.	*3 minutes.*

6 Pour slowly into small cups, leaving a little froth
   on top.

   Serves 4.

   Turkish coffee is very sweet and should not be confused with
ordinary coffee. The sugar, however, may be omitted.

Mulled Wine

Grated rind and juice of 1 lemon
Grated rind and juice of 1 orange
Slices of orange and lemon
$\frac{1}{2}$ nutmeg (broken up)
1-in stick of cinnamon
1 pt ($\frac{1}{2}$ lit) water
4 oz (110 g) sugar
2 bottles red wine

1 Cut a square of butter muslin, 6 x 6in approx.
2 Put fruit rinds, nutmeg and cinnamon in centre
   and tie into a dolly-bag shape with cotton.
3 Place in large suitable bowl with water, sugar
   and wine.

   Cook until it boils,
   8 minutes approx.
   1 hour.

4 Set aside to infuse.
5 Before serving, remove muslin bag and re-heat
   in oven.

   Cook 5 minutes.

6 Add fruit juices.
7 Float orange and lemon slices on top of the
   wine.

   Serves 15.

Appendix: List of Manufacturers

Amana Refrigeration Inc.
per R. E. A. Bott (Wigmore Street) Ltd, 28 Wigmore Street,
London W1A 42H

Apollo Enterprises
2 Grange Road, Thornton Heath, Surrey CR2 8SA

Litton Microwave Ovens
18/19 Regent Parade, Brighton Road, Sutton, Surrey

Macdonalds
Anglesea Road, Woolwich, London SE18 6EG

Merrychef Ltd
Cradock Road, Reading, RG2 0LW

National Panasonic
107 Whitby Road, Slough, Bucks

Philips Electrical Ltd
Century House, Shaftesbury Avenue, London WC2

Sharp Electronics UK Ltd
Sharp House, 107 Hulme Road, Hulme Hall Lane, Manchester M10 8HL

Tappan International Ltd
Daisy Works, 345 Stockport Road, Manchester M13 0LF

Thermador
per R. E. A. Bott (Wigmore Street) Ltd, 28 Wigmore Street,
London W1A 42H

Thorn Domestic Appliances
New Lane, Havant, Hants

Toshiba-Carnair Developments Ltd
Toshiba House, Great South West Road, Feltham, Middx

This is not necessarily an exhaustive list, as new manufacturers are continually coming into this field.

Index

Potato (*contd.*)
  reconstituting instant, 77
Poultry, 42—62
Prawns, 38
  sautéd in brandy and cream, 40
  tomato savoury, 41
Pudding, sponge, 3
  upside-down pineapple, 93
Puffballs, grated cheese, 28
  soup, 27

Quiche, mushroom and aubergine, 81
Quick-stir fry method, 49

Ratatouille, 71, 83
Redcurrant jam, 114
Reheating, 2, 5
Rémoulade, 105
Rhubarb orange whip, 95
  stewed, 94
Rice, 63—70
  boiled, 67
  pilau, 68
  varieties available, 63, 64
Risotto chicken almond, 69
Rognon sauté vin rouge, 57
Rolls, hamburger, 46
Roux, 104
Rum baba, 122
Rusks, 117

Safety factor, 3
  regulations, 6
Salmon chauffage, 32
  cold, 31
  poached, 31
  salad mould, 33
  trout, 29
Sandwiches, hot egg, 85
Sauce, 104—12
  barbecue, 105
  Béchamel, 105
  bolognese, 67, 105
  bread, 105
  cheese, 65
  chocolate, 109
  custard, 109
  lemon, 97
  mushroom, 106

Sauce (*contd.*)
  reconstituting dried mixes, 129
  soubise, 107
  tartare, 105
  tomato, 107
  velouté, 108
  white, 104
Sausages, 59
  quick supper, 59
  and tomato casserole, 60
Scampi, 41
Scotch woodcock, 89
Setting, jam, 114, 115
Shellfish, 5
Shepherd's pie, 48
Shortbread, 126
Shortcrust pastry, 127
Shrimps, 41
Sole Céri, 36
  Dover, 29
  Mornay, 38
  Mornay with prawns, 38
Soups, 21—8
  chicken noodle, 129
  reconstituting dried packet, 129
  spring vegetable, 129
Spaghetti, 64, 67
  bolognese, 67
  cheese, 64
Spare ribs, barbecued, 57
Spinach, cream of, soup, 24
  fresh, 78
  frozen, 79
  purée, 79
Sponge cake yoghurt, 124
  fruit with lemon sauce, 97
  pudding, 3
Steak, 9
  with green peppers, Chinese style, 49
  tenderizing, 45
Stewed dried fruits, 92
Stock cubes, 46
  syrup, 111
Stuffing, 44
  chestnut, 44
Summer casserole, 84
Swedes, freeze-dried, 129
Syrup, stock, 111